A Sourcebook for
Hispanic Literature
and Language

A Sourcebook for Hispanic Literature and Language

Donald W.  *William*
Bleznick

A Selected, Annotated Guide to Spanish and Spanish American Bibliography, Literature, Linguistics, Journals, and Other Source Materials

Temple University Press
Philadelphia

To Rozlyn, Jordan and Susan

Temple University Press, Philadelphia 19122
©1974 by Temple University. All rights reserved
Published 1974
Printed in the United States of America
International Standard Book Number: 0-87722-036-0
Library of Congress Catalog Card Number: 74-77776

Contents

Preface

When the idea for this book came to mind a long time ago, I planned to prepare a practical guide to bibliography and other basic materials which would serve budding and even mature Hispanists in literary and linguistic research. Mindful of the vast array of bibliographic lists and studies that has proliferated in the past several years, I never doubted the need to be *selective* in compiling a manageable vade mecum. The guiding principle that emerged was to identify essential books—occasionally articles when adequate books do not exist—and journals in those areas most central to research in Hispanic literature and language. A corollary aim has been to incorporate current works, many of which are in print and should be available in college and university libraries. Even the fledgling investigator soon learns that one work leads to another, and it is expected that this *Sourcebook* will provide ample resources for research projects ranging from the undergraduate term paper to the doctoral dissertation and beyond.

Motivated by a desire to provide a vehicle for meaningful and rapid reference, I felt it imperative to annotate the books selected. The traditional bibliographic listing, providing only author, title, and date of publication, often fails to offer sufficient clues about a work's contents, and, therefore, I supply succinct descriptions of the scopes of the books included and at times add critical assessments for entries with exceptional merit or some defects. The annotations are generally purposefully brief in order that the reader can determine quickly whether items may be pertinent to his investigation. Very few items are not annotated; this is the case when the title of an entry adequately indicates its contents (and the work has no more than average value) and on the rare occasion when it was not obtainable but its inclusion was deemed necessary for the purpose of having more complete coverage in some areas, particularly the literatures of some Spanish American countries.

The Contents has been carefully designed to set out in a clear and detailed manner all the areas encompassed by this book. One will find the usual items expected in a volume of this kind: works on aims and methods of research, general bibliographic guides and references, style guides, bibliographies of Spanish and Spanish American literature, and

ix

guides to libraries and dissertations. However, this is not merely a bibliography of bibliographies. My purpose is to provide information on various other types of books which students of Hispanic literature and language often need in their work. Accordingly, sections have been introduced to augment the usefulness and uniqueness of this *Sourcebook:* literary dictionaries and encyclopedias; general and specific histories and anthologies of Hispanic literature; books on metrics; bibliographies of literature in translation; a chapter on linguistics, which also devotes a good deal of attention to various types of dictionaries (historical, etymological, grammatical, American Spanish, bilingual, etc.); a guide to 100 journals in the Hispanic field; such helpful references as biographical dictionaries, encyclopedias, handbooks, and works on Hispanic history and philosophy; and current lists of publishers and dealers in Hispanic countries, North America, and Europe.

The date assigned to each book usually indicates the edition examined, and a date in parentheses denotes the first edition. In many cases, when books are merely reprinted they are so marked. It was felt that it would help the reader if the pagination of one-volume works were given, since one would normally expect a vast difference in coverage between a manual of literature that purports to cover a country's literature in 100 pages and one that does so in 500 pages. Standard abbreviations have been used throughout. The numbers found in the Index refer to the entry numbers in the text.

The books chosen in the sections on Spanish and Spanish American literature and anthologies as well as those in linguistics are what *I* consider basic. It is understandable that some may fault me for "glaring" omissions or for including works of little value, but in line with my intent to be selective rather than exhaustive, I have relied on my experience and the opinions of colleagues and students. In general, my cutoff date has been the middle of 1973. Despite my attempts to be current in all sections, it is obvious that I may be unaware of worthwhile publications that have come out lately. Consequently, I invite suggestions for improving the content and organization of this *Sourcebook.*

During the eight or nine years that this book has been in progress, I have been indebted to many colleagues and students. It is impossible to gauge the interest and encouragement of Hensley C. Woodbridge, whose extraordinary bibliographic talents have constantly buttressed my efforts. He has selflessly devoted countless hours to suggesting revisions and additions, finding and supplying new data, and reading at least three versions of this book. I wish to thank my son, Jordan, who assisted me in the final checking of the typescript and the Index. Finally, I am also grateful for the advice and help of Seymour Menton; David S. Zubatsky; H. Tracy Sturcken; John B. Dalbor; Anne S. La Vietes; Edward V. Coughlin; Miriam Baum; María Teresa Martínez; Pilar Concejo; Mark Finch; and Debbie Bruner, who typed the manuscript.

This book largely owes its existence to the love and encouragement of my wife Rozlyn. My children, Jordan and Susan, often unsuspecting their vital roles, have also contributed to creating an environment supportive of this and previous writings.

A Sourcebook for
Hispanic Literature
and Language

1 Aims and Methods of Research

1. **Altick, Richard D.** *The Art of Literary Research.* New York: W. W. Norton & Co., 1963. 276 pp.

   Deals with the spirit of scholarship, textual study, problems of authorship, searching for materials, libraries, note taking, and writing. Bibliography.

2. **Barzun, Jacques, and Henry F. Graff.** *The Modern Researcher.* New York: Harcourt, Brace & World, 1957. ii + 386 pp.

   Illustrates the theory and practice of research and report writing.

3. **Corstius, Jan Brandt.** *Introduction to the Comparative Study of Literature.* New York: Random House, 1968. viii + 212 pp.

   Offers a view of various approaches to the study of Western literature. Extensive bibliographies.

4. **Downs, Robert B.** *How to Do Library Research.* Urbana: University of Illinois Press, 1966. 179 pp.

   Guide to a library and its resources.

5. **Foerster, Norman, et al.** *Literary Scholarship: Its Aims and Methods.* Chapel Hill: University of North Carolina Press, 1941. iv + 269 pp.

   Series of articles by several authors on study of letters, language, literary history, literary criticism, and imaginative writing.

6. **Kayser, Wolfgang.** *Interpretación y análisis de la obra literaria.* 2d ed. Madrid: Gredos, 1961 (1954). 594 pp.

   Extensive treatment that deals with textual study, analysis of a literary work, poetry, rhetorical devices, structure of a literary work, techniques and structures of the different genres, and style. Ample bibliography.

7. **Simón Díaz, José.** *La bibliografía: Conceptos y aplicaciones.* Barcelona: Planeta, 1971. 331 pp.

   Of special interest should be the section entitled "La investigación bibliográfica sobre temas españoles."

8. **Thorpe, James, ed.** *The Aims and Methods of Scholarship in Modern Languages and Literatures.* New York: Modern Language Association, 1963. 69 pp.

Four essays on linguistics, textual criticism, literary history, and literary criticism.

9. ———. *The Relations of Literary Study: Essays on Interdisciplinary Contributions*. New York: Modern Language Association, 1967. xiv + 151 pp.
Seven essays on the relations of literature to history, myth, biography, psychology, sociology, religion, and music.

10. **Van Tieghem, Paul.** *La littérature comparée*. Paris: Armand Colin, 1931. xi + 222 pp.
Presents the theory and method of comparative literature and its history.

11. **Wellek, René, and Austin Warren.** *Teoría literaria*. 4th Spanish ed. Madrid: Gredos, 1966 (1953). 432 pp. Original English version, *Theory of Literature* (New York: Harcourt, Brace, 1942).
Analyzes the natures and functions of literature, literary history, general and comparative literature, the extrinsic approach to literature (biography, psychology, society, and ideas), and the intrinsic approach (literary art, rhythm and meter, style and stylistics, imagery, metaphor, symbol and myth, literary genres, etc.). Many notes and extensive bibliography.

2 General Bibliographic Guides and References

12. **Arnaud, Emile, and Vicente Tusón.** *Guide de bibliographie hispanique.* Toulouse: Privat-Didier, 1967. 353 pp.

Covers wide area including general bibliographies, periodicals, homage volumes, geography, history, fine arts, music, dictionaries, and language. Greatest emphasis given to literature.

13. **Baldensperger, Ferdinand, and Werner P. Friedrich.** *Bibliography of Comparative Literature.* Chapel Hill: University of North Carolina Press, 1950. xxiv + 701 pp. Reprint, New York: Russell & Russell, 1960.

Contains sections on Spanish contributions, including plays and novels, and their influence on writers of other countries. *The Yearbook of General and Comparative Literature* (vols. 1–19) contains an annual supplement to this bibliography.

14. **Besterman, Theodore.** *A World Bibliography of Bibliographies.* 4th rev. ed. Lausanne: Societas Bibliograficas-Lausanne, 1965–66 (1939). 5 vols.

Contains bibliographies through the centuries. Volume 5 has indexes by subject, title, and author.

15. *Bibliographic Index: A Cumulative Bibliography of Bibliographies.* New York: H. W. Wilson & Co., 1938–. Annual supplements.

Entries listed by subject.

16. **Bibliothèque Nationale.** *Catalogue générale des livres imprimés de la Bibliothèque Nationale.* Paris: Imprimerie Nationale, 1897–. In progress: 211 vols. (1972). Supplements published at 5-year intervals; 1960–64, 12 vols. (1965–67).

Mainly a short-title bibliography alphabetized by author.

17. **British Museum.** *General Catalogue of Printed Books.* London: British Museum, 1959–66. 263 vols. 1956–65 Supplement, 50 vols. (1968).

A listing of the holdings of one of the most important libraries in the world.

18. **Collison, Robert L.** *Bibliographies, Subject and National: A*

5

Guide to Their Contents. 3d ed. New York: Hafner Publishing Co., 1968. xviii + 203 pp.

Chapter on language and literature contains material of interest to Hispanists.

19. **Conover, Helen F.** *Current National Bibliographies.* Washington, D.C.: Library of Congress, 1955. vi + 132 pp.

Annotated index of periodical articles, government documents, and directories of periodicals and newspapers. Revision and expansion of *Current National Bibliographies: A List of Sources of Information concerning Current Books of All Countries,* by L. Heyl, first published in 1933.

20. **Downs, Robert B.** *American Library Resources: A Bibliographical Guide.* Chicago: American Library Association, 1951. Pp. 247–49. Also, 1950–61 Supplement (1962), pp. 126–27; and 1961–70 Supplement (1972), pp. 127–28.

Broad coverage. Includes printed library catalogs, union lists of books and serials, special collections, library holdings, and special library reports. Besides linguistics and literature, such areas as philosophy, psychology, religion, and science are covered.

21. *Gesamtverzeichnis ausländischer Zeitschriften und Serien: Hauptband 1939–1958.* Wiesbaden: Otto Harrassowitz, 1963. 2 vols. and supplements for years 1959–66.

Journals, international congresses, and reports of conferences. Includes Spain and Latin America.

22. **Gropp, Arthur E.** *A Bibliography of Latin American Bibliographies.* Metuchen, N.J.: Scarecrow Press, 1968. ix + 515 pp.

Greatly enlarged and updated version of the work of the same title by C. K. Jones published in 1942. Gropp has also published a supplement with the same title (Metuchen, N.J.: Scarecrow Press, 1971; xiii + 277 pp.), which mainly covers the period 1965–69. For both volumes, arrangement of items is by subject, subdivided by country, with occasional subject subdivisions. Has detailed index for each volume.

23. **Lasso de la Vega, Javier.** *Catálogo abreviado de una selección de libros de consulta, referencia, estudio y enseñanza . . . .* Madrid: Junta de Intercambio y Adquisición de Libros para Bibliotecas Públicas, 1953.

More than 11,000 items. All subjects covered, with an excellent representation of Hispanic titles. Bibliographies, criticism, and works are all listed.

24. Malclès, Louise-Noëlle. *Les sources du travail bibliographique.* Geneva: E. Droz, 1950–58. 3 vols. in 4.

General and specialized bibliographies including bibliographical information on languages, grammars, dictionaries, and literature. Hispanic studies included (vol. 2, pp. 324–38).

25. *Modern Language Association International Bibliography of Books and Articles on the Modern Languages and Literatures.* New York: Modern Language Association, 1921–. Published annually.

Fundamental bibliography of journal articles and books. Broadest coverage of annual bibliographies in the field since 1956 when it attempted international coverage. In 1969 it began to appear in a four-volume format which includes such major sections as English, American, and other literatures, linguistics, and pedagogy. Volume 2 covers Romance and Germanic literatures, and volume 3 covers linguistics.

26. *New Serial Titles.* Washington, D.C.: Library of Congress, 1961–. 1950–60, 2 vols. (1961); 1961–65, 3 vols. (1966); 1966–69, 2 vols. (1970). Monthly, then annual, cumulations.

Entries arranged alphabetically by title.

27. Palfrey, Thomas, Joseph Fucilla, and William Holbrook. *A Bibliographical Guide to Romance Languages and Literatures.* 5th ed. Evanston, Ill.: Chandler's, 1964 (1939). 122 pp.

Books listed chronologically according to subject. Occasionally annotated.

28. *Romanische Bibliographie/Bibliographie romane/Romance Bibliography,* 1965–; biennial, 1967–.

New title of the expanded Romance bibliography appearing annually (since 1905) as supplements of the *Zeitschrift für romanische Philologie.* It is a classified bibliography of literature and linguistics with an extremely wide coverage of journals, monographs, and books. The bibliography for 1961–62 was published in four volumes (1965–68); for 1963–64, in three volumes (1968–69). Previous bibliographic supplements of *ZRP* covered 1940–50, 1951–55, 1956–60.

29. *The Romantic Movement Bibliography, 1936–70.* Edited by A. C. Elkins, Jr., and L. J. Forstner. New York: Pierian Press and R. R. Bowker Co., 1973. 7 vols.

Largely descriptive, with occasional annotations of books and articles on English and Continental romanticism. Items previously published in *ELH* (1936–49), *Philological Quarterly* (1950–64), and *English Language Notes* (1965–70).

30. **Sabor, Josefa.** *Manual de fuentes de información; obras de referencia; enciclopedias, diccionarios, bibliografías, biografías,* . . . . 2d ed. Buenos Aires: Kapelusz, 1967 (1957). xv + 342 pp. Annotated listing of general reference works which includes works covering Spain and Latin America, especially Argentina.

31. *Ulrich's International Periodicals Directory: A Classified Guide to a Selected List of Current Periodicals, Foreign and Domestic.* 15th ed. New York: R. R. Bowker Co., 1973–74 (1932). 2,706 pp. Provides basic information about a wide variety of periodicals, including many foreign ones.

32. **UNESCO.** *Bibliographie générale de littérature comparée.* Paris: Librairie M. Didier, 1949–58. 5 vols. Treats such topics as bibliographies, theory, style, literary influences, current movements, and genres.

33. *Union List of Serials in Libraries of the United States and Canada.* 3d ed. New York: H. W. Wilson & Co., 1965. 5 vols. Information on periodical holdings of more than 600 libraries.

34. **U.S. Library of Congress.** *A Catalog of Books Represented by Library of Congress Printed Cards Issued to July 31, 1942.* Ann Arbor, Mich.: J. W. Edwards, 1942. 167 vols. Supplements: 1942–47, 42 vols. (1948); 1948–52, 24 vols. (1953).

35. ———. *Library of Congress and National Union Catalog Author Lists, 1942–1962.* Detroit: Gale Research, 1969–. A cumulative author list.

36. ———. *Library of Congress Catalog—Books: Subjects, a Cumulative List of Works Represented by Library of Congress Printed Cards.* Washington, D.C., 1950–. Cumulative supplements for 1950–54, 1955–59, 1960–64, 1965–69. Quarterly, annual, and 5-year cumulations.

37. ———. *The National Union Catalog, 1952–55 Imprints: An Author List Representing Library of Congress Printed Cards and Titles Reported by Other American Libraries.* Ann Arbor, Mich.: J. W. Edwards, 1961–. 30 vols. Supplements: 1953–57 (1958); 1958–62 (1963); 1963 (1964); 1963–67 (1969).

38. ———. *The National Union Catalog, Pre-1956 Imprints.* London: Mansell, 1968–.

A cumulative author list representing Library of Congress printed cards and titles reported by other American libraries. This represents an attempt to make one union list of Library of Congress entries and those of other collections published before 1956.

39. Walford, Albert John. *Guide to Reference Materials.* 2d ed. London: Library Association, 1970 (1959). 585 pp.

Lists recent reference books by country and subject. Contains many items for Spain and Spanish America in sections on bibliography, language, and literature. Emphasis is on items published in Britain.

40. Winchell, Constance M. *Guide to Reference Books.* 8th ed. Chicago: American Library Association, 1967 (1902). xx + 741 pp. Supplements compiled by Eugene P. Sheehy: 1965–66 (1968); 1967–68 (1970); 1969–70 (1972).

Very useful, well-organized reference.

41. *The Year's Work in Modern Language Studies.* Cambridge: Modern Humanities Research Association, 1931–40; 1950–.

Annual critical survey of work done in modern languages and literatures. Indexes of subjects and names.

42. Zamarriego, Tomás. *Enciclopedia de orientación bibliográfica.* Barcelona: Juan Flors, 1964–65. 4 vols.

International in scope but with heavy concentration on Spanish, especially humanities and religion. Fifth part of volume 3 deals with literature. Each entry is well annotated.

3   Style Guides

43. **Hurt, Peyton.** *Bibliography and Footnotes.* 2d ed., revised and enlarged by Mary L. Hurt Richmon. Berkeley and Los Angeles: University of California Press, 1963 (1949). 166 pp.

Demonstrates the making of a bibliography and the use of footnotes. Also contains a section on style.

44. **Parker, William R.** *The MLA Style Sheet.* 2d ed. New York: Modern Language Association, 1970 (1951). 48 pp.

A style sheet accepted by many journals, university presses, language departments, and graduate schools.

45. **Turabian, Kate L.** *A Manual for Writers of Term Papers, Theses, and Dissertations.* 4th ed. Chicago: University of Chicago Press, 1973 (1955). 208 pp.

Explains and illustrates all phases of writing and typing a formal paper. Follows the University of Chicago Press's *Manual of Style.*

46. **University of Chicago Press.** *A Manual of Style.* 12th ed. Chicago: University of Chicago Press, 1969 (1906). 546 pp.

Exhaustive coverage of all questions of style. Standard reference.

4   Bibliographies of Hispanic Literature

For bibliographies besides those listed below, consult chapter 13 (pp. 130–49) for bibliographies included in major journals in the Hispanic field. Especially useful are the bibliographies in the *Nueva revista de filología hispánica* (Mexico, 1947–) for literature and linguistics of Spain; the *Revista de filología hispánica* (Buenos Aires and New York, 1939–46), superseded by *NRFH,* for Hispanic literature and linguistics; the *Revista hispánica moderna* (New York, 1935–68) for Spanish American literature and linguistics; the *Revista de filología española* (Madrid, 1914–) for Spanish linguistics and literature; the *Revista de literatura* (Madrid, 1952–) for Spanish literature; and *La torre* (Puerto Rico, 1953–) on Hispanic literature.

Spain and Spanish America

47. *Bibliografía histórica de España e Hispanoamérica.* Barcelona: Teide, 1953–. Three numbers published annually.

    Annotated listing of books and articles. While this is general bibliography, entries pertaining to literature are numerous.

48. Foster, David W., and Virginia Ramos Foster. *Manual of Hispanic Bibliography.* Seattle: University of Washington Press, 1970. xi + 206 pp.

    Comprehensive bibliographic guide to general bibliographies of Spanish and Spanish American literatures. Also includes guides to libraries and collections, periodical literature, and theses. For Spanish America, entries are listed according to country and by periods. Index included.

49. Golden, Herbert H., and Seymour O. Simches. *Modern Iberian Language and Literature: A Bibliography of Homage Studies.* Cambridge, Mass.: Harvard University Press, 1958. x + 184 pp. Reprint, Millwood, N.Y.: Kraus Reprints, 1971.

    Lists studies in homage works up to 1956. Concerned primarily with the Catalonian, Portuguese, and Spanish languages and literatures, with some articles relating to Spanish America and Brazil.

50. Grismer, Raymond L. *A Bibliography of Articles and Essays on*

the Literature of Spain and Spanish America. Minneapolis, Minn.: Perine Book Co., 1935. 423 pp.
The scope of this work is from the Middle Ages to the twentieth century. Sections on dialects, individual American countries, and interrelationships of different languages.

51. ———. *Bibliography of the Drama of Spain and Spanish America*. Minneapolis, Minn.: Burgess-Beckwith, 1967–69. 2 vols.
Alphabetical listing by critic. Contains a dramatist-critic index.

52. ———. *A New Bibliography of the Literatures of Spain and Spanish America*. Minneapolis, Minn.: Perine Book Co., 1941–46. 7 vols.
Listing is by author, but covers only from "a" to "cez." Books and magazines in subjects other than literature are included.

53. Hatzfeld, Helmut A. *A Critical Bibliography of the New Stylistics Applied to the Romance Literatures, 1953–1965*. Chapel Hill: University of North Carolina Press, 1966. 183 pp. Spanish version, *Bibliografía crítica de la nueva estilística aplicada a las literaturas románicas* (Madrid: Gredos, 1955).
Contains almost 1,900 concisely annotated entries. This meticulously organized work covers such categories as theory of style and stylistics, *explication de texte,* translations, stylistic parallels and variants, style and structure of literary works, aspects of style, and motifs. It also has two useful indexes: one of style investigators, and the other of authors, titles, and terms. It continues the author's work of the same title and publisher (1953, reprinted by Johnson Reprint Corp.) which covers the years 1900–1952.

54. *Libros en venta en Hispanoamérica y España*. Directed by Mary C. Turner. New York: R. R. Bowker Co., 1964. 1,891 pp. Supplements for years 1964–66, 1967–68, 1969–70, and 1971.
Author, title, and subject listings of books in print in Spain and 20 countries of Spanish America. Contains an extensive list of publishers of Spanish books. Bowker's monthly *Fichero bibliográfico hispanoamericano* (see no. 86) features listings of newly published Spanish-language books.

55. Palau y Dulcet, Antonio. *Manual del librero hispanoamericano: Inventario bibliográfico de la producción científica y literaria de España y de la América latina*. Barcelona: Librería Anticuaria de A. Palau, 1948–72. 24 vols. Vol. 24 (1972): "Tow" to "Valderrama."
Most complete bibliography of Spanish publications up to the

twentieth century. Some noteworthy editions of this century are listed.

56. Schanzer, George O. *Russian Literature in the Hispanic World: A Bibliography.* Toronto: University of Toronto Press, 1972. 312 pp.

Listing of Spanish collections and anthologies of Russian literature, individual translations, criticisms both general and specific, and sections of semiliterary writings from 1838 to 1965. Some annotations.

57. Simón Díaz, José. *Bibliografía de la literatura hispánica.* Madrid: Consejo Superior de Investigaciones Científicas, 1950–. 10 vols.

Volume 1: literary history, collections of texts, anthologies, monographs, comparative literature; Catalan, Galician, and Basque literatures with many of the same major divisions. Volume 2: bibliography of bibliographies, biography and biobibliography, general bibliography, catalogs of libraries, catalogs of periodicals, catalogs of archives, indexes to periodical publications, general and partial literature bibliographies, bibliographies of other subjects. Same for Catalan and Basque. Volume 3, in two parts: medieval literature. Volumes 4–10: Golden Age Spanish literature (volume 10: "F" to "Gondino").

58. Thompson, Lawrence S. *A Bibliography of Spanish Plays on Microcards.* Hamden, Conn.: Shoe String Press, 1968. viii + 490 pp.

Six thousand Spanish, Catalonian, and Spanish American plays from the sixteenth century to the present, based on holdings in the University of Kentucky Library.

59. Vindel, Francisco. *Manual gráfico-descriptivo del bibliófilo hispanoamericano, 1475–1850.* Madrid: Imprenta Góngora, 1930–34. 12 vols.

Reproductions of covers and fragments of several thousand books. Brief descriptions.

Spain

General

60. Antonio, Nicolás. *Bibliotheca hispana nova.* 2d ed. Madrid: Viuda de Ibarra, 1783–88 (1672). 2 vols. Facsimile ed., Turin: Bottega d'Erasmo, 1963. 2 vols.

Written in Latin. Writers covered from 1500 to 1684. This first bibliography of Spanish literature is a basic tool for the study of Peninsular literature.

61. ———. *Bibliotheca hispana vetus*. 2d ed. Madrid: Viuda de Ibarra, 1788 (1696). 2 vols. Facsimile ed., Turin: Bottega d'Erasmo, 1963. 467 pp.

Written in Latin. From Augustine Empire to 1500. This second bibliography of Spanish literature is a basic tool for the study of early Peninsular literature.

62. Barrera y Leirado, Cayetano Alberto de la. *Catálogo bibliográfico y biográfico del teatro antiguo español, desde sus orígenes hasta mediados del siglo XVIII*. Madrid: M. Rivadeneyra, 1860. 2 vols. Facsimile eds., Madrid: Támesis, 1968; Madrid: Gredos, 1969.

A short biographical sketch of each author with a chronological list of his works. Various appendixes are included. Valuable source of information for study of early theater.

63. Brown, Reginald F. *La novela española, 1700–1850*. Madrid: Servicio de Publicaciones del Ministerio de Educación Nacional, 1953. 221 pp.

The main section is an annotated chronological listing of novels.

64. Foulché-Delbosc, Raymond. *Bibliographie hispanique*. New York: Hispanic Society of America, 1905–17. 13 vols.

Listing of books, pamphlets, and articles on languages, literatures, and histories of Spanish, Catalan, and Portuguese. Volumes for 1912–14 contain *Bibliographie hispano-française* of Foulché-Delbosc; volumes for 1915–17 have *Bibliographie hispano-grecque,* in collaboration with Emile Legrand.

65. Foulché-Delbosc, Raymond, and L. Barrau-Dihigo. *Manuel de l'Hispanisant*. New York: G. P. Putnam's Sons, 1920–25. 2 vols. Facsimile ed., Millwood, N.Y.: Kraus Reprints, 1959.

Essential bibliographical guide.

66. Haebler, Konrad. *Bibliografía ibérica del siglo XV: Enumeración de todos los libros impresos en España y Portugal hasta el año 1500 con notas críticas por Conrado Haebler*. New York: Burt Franklin Reprints, 1960 (1903–17). 2 vols.

Lengthy annotations of more than 700 works.

67. Kayserling, M. *Biblioteca española-portugueza-judaica: Dictionnaire bibliographique des auteurs juifs, de leurs ouvrages espagnoles et des oeuvres sur et contre les juifs et le judaisme avec un aperçu sur la littérature des juifs espagnoles et une collection des* *proverbes espagnoles.* Reprint. New York: Ktav Publishing House, 1971 (1890). 272 pp.

Dictionary of Jewish Iberian authors from early times to the nineteenth century.

68. **Laurenti, Joseph L.** *Bibliografía de la literatura picaresca: Desde sus orígenes hasta el presente.* Metuchen, N.J.: Scarecrow Press, 1973. 280 pp.

Covers 19 important picaresque works, citing editions, translations, and critical studies in major European languages. Also includes studies on the word "picaresque," studies on the picaresque in the Golden Age, and studies on the influences of picaresque literature and its relation to other forms of literature.

69. **McCready, Warren T.** *Bibliografía temática de estudios sobre el teatro español antiguo.* Toronto: University of Toronto Press, 1966. xix + 445 pp.

Studies published between 1850 and 1950, dealing with the Spanish theater from early times to the beginning of the eighteenth century.

70. **Penney, Clara Louise.** *Printed Books, 1468–1700, in the Hispanic Society of America.* 2d ed. New York: Hispanic Society of America, 1965 (1929, 1938). xlii + 614 pp.

A short-title alphabetical listing.

71. **Pérez Pastor, Cristóbal.** *Bibliografía madrileña o descripción de las obras impresas en Madrid (1566–1625).* Madrid: Huérfanos, 1891–1907. 3 vols.

Arranged chronologically and alphabetically by author. Useful annotations. A basic bibliography for the period covered.

72. **Serís, Homero.** *Manual de bibliografía de la literatura española.* Syracuse: Centro de Estudios Hispánicos, 1948–54. 1,086 pp. in 2 pts.

Covers general works, biobibliographical studies, literary genres, culture, art, and folklore.

73. **Simón Díaz, José.** *Manual de bibliografía de la literatura española.* 2d ed. Barcelona: Gustavo Gili, 1966 (1963). 603 + 100 pp. 2d supplement (1972). 198 pp.

The 1966 edition reproduces the original and includes a supplement for the years 1962–64. Lists studies of all aspects of Spanish literature and a few linguistic studies. Author and subject indexes. Probably the most useful one-volume bibliography of Spanish literature.

74. Stubbings, H. U. *Renaissance Spain in Its Literary Relations with England and France: A Critical Bibliography.* Nashville, Tenn.: Vanderbilt University Press, 1969. 138 pp.

Annotated bibliography of 364 items covering books, monographs, and articles. Extensive index.

75. Thomas, Henry. *Short-Title Catalogue of Spanish, Spanish-American, and Portuguese Books Printed before 1601 in the British Museum.* Reprint. London: British Museum, 1966 (1921). xv + 169 pp. (See no. 1007.)

Arranged alphabetically in three sections: Spanish, Spanish-American, and Portuguese.

Serial

76. *Bibliografía española.* Madrid: Ministerio de Educación Nacional: Dirección General de Archivos y Bibliotecas, 1958–.

Annual general bibliography based on copyright receipts in the Biblioteca Nacional. Index of authors, titles, and subjects, and lists of publishers, series, and periodicals.

77. *Bibliotheca hispana: Revista de información y orientación bibliográfica.* Madrid: Consejo Superior de Investigaciones Científicas, 1943–.

Annual bibliography covering wide range of subject matter, including philology and literature.

78. *Boletín del depósito legal de obras impresas.* Madrid: Ministerio de Educación Nacional: Dirección General de Archivos y Bibliotecas, 1958–.

Lists all books printed in Spain.

79. *El libro español.* Madrid: Instituto Nacional del Libro Español, 1958–.

Classified monthly listing of current and forthcoming books. Also contains brief articles on the literary world.

Spanish America

General

80. Anderson, Robert Roland. *Spanish American Modernism: A Selected Bibliography.* Tucson: University of Arizona Press, 1970. 167 pp.

Critical studies on 18 authors plus a section of general studies on the movement as a whole.

81. *Anuario hispanoamericano.* Madrid: Mundus, 1953–.

Includes literature and culture among broad range of subjects covered.

82. Behar, D., and R. Behar. *Libros antiguos y modernos referentes a América y España.* Buenos Aires: Librería Panamericana, 1947. 371 pp.

Covers history, periodicals, bibliographies, and indigenous languages. Some annotations.

83. Berliner, J. J., and staff. *Bibliography of Latin America.* New York: J. J. Berliner, 1935–40. 6 vols.

Each volume gives chronologically arranged bibliographic information on general cultural material.

84. Bryant, Shasta M. *A Selective Bibliography of Bibliographies of Hispanic American Literature.* Washington, D.C.: Pan American Union, 1966. 48 pp.

Almost 400 items on general and specialized bibliographies.

85. Dorn, Georgette M., comp. *Latin America, Spain, and Portugal: An Annotated Bibliography of Paperback Books.* Washington, D.C.: Library of Congress, 1971. 180 pp.

Listing of 1,512 inexpensive paperbacks. Includes a section on grammars, dictionaries, and textbooks.

86. *Fichero bibliográfico hispanoamericano.* Directed by Mary C. Turner. New York: R. R. Bowker Co., 1961–. Published monthly.

Lists new books published in Spanish America. Classified arrangement by suggested Library of Congress number. Author and title indexes as well as addresses of publishers are included. (See no. 54.)

87. Geoghegan, Abel Rodolfo. *Obras de referencia de América latina: Repertorio selectivo y anotado de enciclopedias, diccionarios, bibliografías, repertorios biográficos, catálogos, guías, anuarios, índices, ...* Buenos Aires: Crisol, 1965. xxiii + 280 pp.

Annotates 2,694 works of reference, including books as well as articles from more than 165 periodical publications.

88. Grismer, Raymond L. *A Reference Index to 12,000 Spanish American Authors: A Guide to the Literature of Spanish America.* New York: H. W. Wilson & Co., 1939. 150 pp. Reprint, Detroit: Blaine Ethridge Books, 1971.

Indexes more than 125 reference sets, encyclopedias, and the like, covering writers in all genres.

89. Gropp, Arthur. *Bibliografía sobre las bibliotecas nacionales de los países latinoamericanos y sus publicaciones.* Washington, D.C.: Pan American Union, 1960. iv + 58 pp.

————. *Bibliography of Latin American Bibliographies.* See no. 22.

90. Hebblethwaite, Frank P. *A Bibliographical Guide to the Spanish American Theater.* Washington, D.C.: Pan American Union, 1969. viii + 84 pp.

Books and articles divided by country. Many items are annotated.

91. *Index to Latin American Periodical Literature, 1929–1960.* Boston: G. K. Hall & Co., 1962. 8 vols. 1961–65 Supplement (1968). (See no. 886.)

Arranged alphabetically by author, title, and subject with coverage of around 1,700 periodicals. Some brief annotations.

92. Leguizamón, Julio. *Bibliografía general de la literatura hispanoamericana.* Buenos Aires: Editoriales Reunidas, 1954. 213 pp.

Anthologies of and studies on Spanish American literature covering all countries and all genres. Author index. Not annotated.

93. Lohman Villena, Guillermo, Luis J. Cisneros, Julio Ortega, and Horacio J. Becco. *Bibliografía general de la literatura latinoamericana.* Paris: UNESCO, 1972. 187 pp.

Annotated bibliography (finished around 1967) that covers the colonial period, the nineteenth century, and the twentieth century. Contains bibliographies of bibliographies, critical studies, literary histories, collections of essays, and proceedings of literary congresses.

94. Medina, José Toribio. *Biblioteca hispanoamericana (1493–1810).* Facsimile ed. Santiago de Chile, 1958–62 (1898–1907). 7 vols.

Includes works by Americans and Spaniards in chronological order.

95. Mesa, Rosa Quintero, comp. *Latin American Serial Documents.* Ann Arbor, Mich.: R. R. Bowker Co., 1968–. 19 vols. projected.

Will provide bibliographic data on thousands of serials from each Latin American nation. Indicates United States library holdings. As of 1972, the volumes on Argentina, Bolivia, Colombia, Brazil, Cuba, and Mexico were published.

96. Okinshevich, Leo. *Latin America in Soviet Writings: A Bibliography.* Baltimore: Johns Hopkins Press, 1966. 2 vols.

Updates and expands earlier work, *Latin America in Soviet Writings,* published by Library of Congress. Covers total geographical area and all material.

97. Pan American Union, Columbus Memorial Library. *List of Books Accessioned and Periodical Articles Indexed.* Boston: G. K. Hall & Co., 1953–70.

Annual listing of cultural aspects of Latin American life.

98. Payró, Roberto P. *Historias de la literatura americana: Guía bibliográfica.* Washington, D.C.: Pan American Union, 1950. 59 pp.

Includes some journal articles.

99. *Polibiblón: Bibliografía acumulativa argentina e hispanoamericana.* Buenos Aires, 1947–.

Includes Argentine, Spanish American, and Spanish books and reviews. Entries are by subject and some are annotated.

100. Rela, Walter. *Guía bibliográfica de la literatura hispanoamericana desde el siglo XIX hasta 1970.* Buenos Aires: Casa Pardo, 1971. 613 pp.

Contains 6,023 items. Unannotated, well indexed, but still difficult to use because many sections are arranged by the author of the work, rather than by the author written about. No articles listed.

101. Rodríguez, Mario, and Vincent C. Peloso. *A Guide for the Study of Culture in Central America: Humanities and Social Sciences.* Washington, D.C.: Pan American Union, Division of Philosophy and Letters, 1968. 88 pp.

Lists 934 reference works, documentary sets, cultural journals, and books and articles on the humanities and social sciences.

102. Sánchez, Luis Alberto. *Repertorio bibliográfico de la literatura latinoamericana.* Vol. 1, Santiago de Chile: Talleres Gráficos, Encuadernación Hispano Suiza, 1955. Vol. 2, Lima: Universidad Mayor de San Marcos, 1957. Vol. 3, Santiago de Chile: Universidad de Chile, 1962.

Includes literary history, criticism, and anthologies. Annotated entries and bibliographic information. Volume 1 covers Central America and Argentina, volume 2 includes Bolivia and Brazil, and volume 3 is devoted to Chile and Colombia.

103. Topete, J. M. *A Working Bibliography of Latin American Litera-*

ture. St. Augustine, Fla.: Inter-American Bibliographical Association, 1952. 162 pp.

All countries covered. Divided into many categories according to subject.

104. Watson, Alice G. H. *A Guide to Reference Materials of Colombia, Ecuador, and Venezuela Useful in Social Science and Humanities.* Metuchen, N.J.: Scarecrow Press, 1971. 279 pp.

Contains evaluations of 894 current and retrospective bibliographies and reference works.

105. Zimmerman, Irene. *Current National Bibliographies of Latin America: A State of the Art Study.* Gainesville: University of Florida, Center for Latin American Studies, 1971. 139 pp.

Covers the status of the current Latin American national bibliographies in descriptive form, with useful summaries for each country. Also has an appendix on the Seminars on the Acquisition of Latin American Library Materials (SALALM) and a selective bibliography on serials, books, articles, and papers.

National (alphabetized by country or region)

Argentina

106. Becco, Horacio Jorge. *Bibliografías de bibliografías literarias argentinas.* Washington, D.C.: Secretaría General de la Organización de los Estados Americanos, 1972. 89 pp.

Annotated bibliography of literary Argentine bibliographies together with more than 300 bibliographies on individual authors, themes, genres, and related subjects, and also 18 general Latin American bibliographies.

107. ———. *Fuentes para el estudio de la literatura argentina.* Buenos Aires: Centro Editor de América Latina, 1968. 62 pp.

Divided into nine sections: bibliography, literary history, literary criticism, biographies, magazines and newspapers, theater, anthologies, reference works, and literary collections.

108. *Bibliografía argentina de artes y letras.* Directed by Augusto Raúl Cortázar. Buenos Aires: Fondo Nacional de las Artes, 1959–. Cumulative index for 1959–63 in no. 20 (1963). Cumulative alphabetical index for 1964–68 and cumulative subject index for nos. 1–40 (1959–69) in no. 39/40 (1969). Appears quarterly.

Literary and cultural cumulative bibliography. List includes books, scholarly publications, literary criticism, and the like. Special bibliographic numbers are often devoted to material on single authors or topics; for example, the issue corresponding to number 29/30 (1966) has a 48-page bibliography entitled "Cuento fantástico argentino en el siglo XX."

109. *Biblos.* Directed by Gonzalo Losada. Buenos Aires: Cámara Argentina del Libro, 1943–. Published bimonthly.

Coverage of publications by main Argentine publishers. Bibliographic data and brief reviews.

110. Foster, David W., and Virginia Ramos Foster. *Research Guide to Argentine Literature.* Metuchen, N.J.: Scarecrow Press, 1970. 146 pp.

Studies on more than 40 major Argentine literary figures (excluding Alberdi, Rojas, and Sarmiento). Sections on bibliographic sources, research on general and specific topics, and journals. Comprises 1,000 entries, which are indexed. Selective and not annotated.

111. Geoghegan, Abel Rodolfo. *Bibliografía de bibliografías argentinas (1807–1970).* Preliminary ed. Buenos Aires: Casa Pardo, 1970. 130 pp.

A selective listing that includes 452 bibliographies, most of which are annotated. Contains sections on general works and works in such fields as philosophy, religion, and social sciences. There are 30 works listed for literature and 14 for linguistics.

112. Pepe, Luz E. A. *La crítica teatral argentina (1880–1962).* Buenos Aires: Fondo Nacional de las Artes, 1966. 78 pp.

Contains 782 entries, many of which are annotated. List of companies, friends of theater, and experimental theaters.

Polibiblón. See no. 99.

113. Sabor, Josefa E., and Lydia H. Revello. *Bibliografía básica de obras de referencia de artes y letras para la Argentina.* Buenos Aires: Fondo Nacional de las Artes, 1968. 78 pp.

Two hundred forty-eight items are annotated.

Bolivia

114. *Bibliografía boliviana.* Cochabamba: Los Amigos del Libro, 1962–. Published annually.

An alphabetical listing of books and pamphlets published in Bolivia. Contains a separate bibliography of books on Bolivia written abroad. Title and subject indexes and a list of publishers and printers.

115. Costa de la Torre, Arturo. *Catálogo de la bibliografía boliviana.* La Paz: Universidad Mayor de San Andrés, 1969–73. 2 vols. Vol. 1, 1,255 pp.; vol. 2, 1,250 pp.

Lists books and pamphlets for 1900–1963. Includes more than 3,000 Bolivian authors with some 8,700 bibliographic entries. Extensive introductory section (1:1–237) provides a comprehensive survey of Bolivian bibliography.

116. Siles Guevara, Juan. *Bibliografía de bibliografías bolivianas.* La Paz: Ministerio de Cultura, Información y Turismo, Imprenta del Estado, 1969. 38 pp. 2d ed., La Paz, 1970 (*Estudios andinos* 1, no. 1:149–70).

The second edition contains 120 entries, 17 more than the first. Presents a fairly complete panorama of the current state of bibliographic activities in Bolivia. No author index.

Central America

117. Doyle, Henry Grattan. *A Tentative Bibliography of the Belles-Lettres of the Republics of Central America.* Cambridge, Mass.: Harvard University Press, 1935. 136 pp.

Divided by country. A supplement on periodicals and newspapers is included.

118. Peraza Sarausa, Fermín. *Bibliografía de Centroamérica y del Caribe, 1956–1959.* Havana: Agrupación Bibliográfica Cubana José Toribio Medina and Archivos y Bibliotecas de España, 1958–61. 4 vols.

Books and pamphlets dealing with the cultures of Caribbean countries.

Rodríguez and Peloso. *Guide for the Study of Culture in Central America.* See no. 101.

Chile

119. Castillo, Homero, and Raúl Silva Castro. *Historia bibliográfica de la novela chilena.* Mexico: Ediciones de Andrea, 1961. 214 pp.

Authors are listed alphabetically, and titles are in chronological order.

120. Castillo, Homero. *La literatura chilena en los Estados Unidos de América.* Santiago: Biblioteca Nacional, 1963. 127 pp.

Covers publications in the United States of texts, anthologies, translations, and criticism of Chilean literature. About 1,500 entries.

121. **Durán Cerda, Julio.** *Repertorio del teatro chileno: Bibliografía, obras inéditas y estrenos.* Santiago: Instituto de Literatura Chilena, 1962. 247 pp.

Covers theater in Chile since 1910.

122. **Felíu Cruz, Guillermo.** *Historia de las fuentes de la bibliografía chilena: Ensayo crítico.* Santiago: Biblioteca Nacional, 1966–67. 3 vols.

First scholarly study on the history of Chilean bibliography. Covers such outstanding nineteenth-century bibliographers as Medina, Bello, and Vicuña Mackenna.

123. **Goić, Cedomil.** *Bibliografía de la novela chilena del siglo XX.* Santiago: Editorial Universitaria, 1962. 168 pp.

The Chilean novel from 1910 to 1961, arranged chronologically.

124. **Rela, Walter.** *Contribución a la bibliografía del teatro chileno, 1804–1960.* Montevideo: Universidad de la República, 1960. 51 pp.

Lists 895 items with author and title index.

125. *Servicio bibliográfico chileno.* Santiago: Zamorano y Caperan, 1940–71. Published monthly at the beginning, and then quarterly.

Unannotated listing of books published in Chile.

Colombia

126. *Anuario bibliográfico colombiano "Rubén Pérez Ortiz."* Bogota: Instituto Caro y Cuervo, Departamento de Bibliografía, 1951–. Published annually.

A publication containing articles, books, pamphlets, periodicals, and government publications. Indexes of authors, translations, publishers, and bookstores.

127. *Bibliografía colombiana.* Directed by Fermín Peraza Sarausa. Gainesville, Fla., 1961–68. 13 vols.

Alphabetical listing of books published in Colombia and also books on Colombia published abroad.

128. **Giraldo Jaramillo, Gabriel.** *Bibliografía de bibliografías colombianas.* 2d ed., revised by Rubén Pérez Ortiz. Bogota: Instituto Caro y Cuervo, 1960. 204 pp.

Annotated bibliography of general bibliographies, catalogs of libraries, biographies of individuals, and a short bibliography of Colombian literature.

129. Orjuela, Héctor H. *Las antologías poéticas de Colombia: Estudio y bibliografía.* Bogota: Instituto Caro y Cuervo, 1966. 514 pp.

Study of 147 anthologies published in Chile and 242 foreign anthologies.

130. ———. *Bibliografía de la poesía colombiana.* Bogota: Instituto Caro y Cuervo, 1971. 486 pp.

Alphabetical arrangement of principal editions and pamphlets up to 1970.

131. ———. *Fuentes generales para el estudio de la literatura colombiana: Guía bibliográfica.* Bogota: Instituto Caro y Cuervo, 1968. x1 + 863 pp.

Several thousand items. Division by subject and then listing by author. Indicates location of items.

Costa Rica

132. *Anuario bibliográfico costarricense.* San José: Asociación Costarricense de Bibliotecarios, 1956–. Published every few years.

Cumulative and national bibliography.

133. *Boletín bibliográfico.* San José: Imprenta Nacional, 1946–55.

Continued by the *Anuario bibliográfico costarricense* (see no. 132).

134. Menton, Seymour. *El cuento costarricense: Estudio, antología y bibliografía.* Mexico: Ediciones de Andrea, 1964. 184 pp.

Bibliography until 1960.

Cuba

135. *Anuario bibliográfico cubano.* Havana: Alfa, 1938–66.

Until 1958 arranged by authors and by subject, then by author. Succeeded by *Revolutionary Cuba: A Bibliographical Guide* (see no. 139).

136. Montes Huidobro, Matías, and Yara González. *Bibliografía crítica de la poesía cubana.* Madrid: Plaza Mayor Ediciones, 1972. 136 pp.

Covers the years 1959–71. Poets listed in alphabetical order with their works and comments on them.

137. Peraza Sarausa, Fermín. *Bibliografía cubana, complementos 1937–1961.* Gainesville: University of Florida Libraries, 1966. viii + 233 pp.

Alphabetical listing of the addenda to the first 25 volumes of the *Anuario bibliográfico cubano* (see no. 135). Includes subject index of the nearly 4,000 items.

138. ———. *Bibliografías cubanas*. Washington, D.C.: Library of Congress Hispanic Foundation, 1945. xiv + 58 pp.

    Contains 485 entries, divided into general, subject, and personal bibliographies. Index of authors and works.

139. *Revolutionary Cuba: A Bibliographical Guide*. Coral Gables, Fla.: University of Miami Press, 1966–. Published annually.

    An alphabetical listing of books, pamphlets, serials, and government publications. Has an author-subject index.

Dominican Republic

140. *Anuario bibliográfico dominicano*. Santo Domingo: Luis Sánchez Adújar, 1947–. Published irregularly.

    Listing of books with author index.

Ecuador

141. *Bibliografía ecuatoriana*. Quito: Biblioteca Municipal, 1959–.

142. Chaves, Alfredo. *Fuentes principales de la bibliografía ecuatoriana*. Quito: Casa de la Cultura Ecuatoriana, 1958. 24 pp.

    Treats primarily fields of literature, criticism, and journalism.

El Salvador

143. *Bibliografía salvadoreña: Lista preliminar por autores*. San Salvador: Biblioteca Nacional, 1953. 430 pp.

    Occasional brief annotations.

Guatemala

144. *Anuario bibliográfico guatemalteco*. Guatemala: Biblioteca Nacional, 1960–. Published annually.

    Listing of books, pamphlets, and periodicals; also contains a list of principal presses and publishing houses.

145. Valenzuela G., director. *Bibliografía guatemalteca y catálogo general de libros, folletos, periódicos, revistas, ...* Guatemala: Tipografía Nacional, 1933–.

    Chronological listing of Guatemalan publications from 1660 to the present. Majority of volumes date from 1961.

Honduras

146. García, Miguel Angel. *Anuario bibliográfico hondureño, 1961–1971*. Tegucigalpa: Banco Central de Honduras, 1973. 512 pp.

    List of publications for each year arranged by subject, followed by a list of government documents for that year. Data are also provided on Honduran newspapers and periodicals.

147. ———. *Bibliografía hondureña, 1620–1930.* Tegucigalpa: Banco Central de Honduras, 1971. 203 pp.

Items are arranged chronologically.

148. ———. *Bibliografía hondureña, 1931–1960.* Tegucigalpa: Banco Central de Honduras, 1972. 230 pp.

Items are arranged chronologically.

Mexico

149. *Bibliografía mexicana.* Mexico: Biblioteca Nacional, 1967–. Published six times a year.

Classified bibliography of current Mexican books.

150. *Boletín bibliográfico mexicano.* Mexico: Porrúa, 1940–. Published bimonthly.

Cumulative bibliography arranged alphabetically by subject. Contains book reviews, new notes, and publishers' advertisements.

151. Lamb, Ruth S. *Bibliografía del teatro mexicano del siglo XX.* Mexico: Ediciones de Andrea, 1962. 141 pp.

A brief history of the Mexican theater introduces the works. Alphabetical arrangement by author. Short bibliography of criticism on Mexican theater.

152. Leal, Luis. *Bibliografía del cuento mexicano.* Mexico: Ediciones de Andrea, 1958. 162 pp.

Alphabetical author listing of the short story since the eighteenth century. Includes titles of books as well as short stories published in newspapers and magazines.

153. Martínez, José Luis. *Literatura mexicana siglo XX, 1910–1949.* Mexico: Robredo, 1949–50. 2 vols.

Volume 2 contains a general bibliography and bibliographies of Mexican literature, anthologies, critical studies, literary journals, and Spanish poetry in Mexico (1939–49).

154. Millares Carlo, Agustín, and José Ignacio Mantecón. *Ensayo de una bibliografía de bibliografías mexicanas (la imprenta, el libro, las bibliotecas, . . .).* Mexico: Panamericana, 1943. xvi + 224 pp.

Partially annotated. Includes publications in the United States, Europe, and Latin America.

155. Ocampo de Gómez, Aurora Maura. *Literatura mexicana contemporánea: Biobibliografía crítica.* Mexico: Universidad Nacional Autónoma de México, 1965. 325 pp.

Covers the principal figures in criticism, poetry, prose fiction, and drama. Evaluative notes on each writer's works.

Panama

156. Doyle, Henry Grattan. *A Tentative Bibliography of the Belles-Lettres of Panama.* Cambridge, Mass.: Harvard University Press, 1934. 21 pp.

General works plus listing by authors.

157. King, Charles A. "Apuntes para una bibliografía de la literatura de Panamá." *Inter-American Review of Bibliography* 14 (July–September 1964): 262–302.

Sections arranged by genres.

Paraguay

158. Fernández-Caballero, Carlos F. S. *The Paraguayan Bibliography: A Retrospective and Enumerative Bibliography of Printed Works of Paraguayan Authors.* Washington, D.C.: Paraguay Arandú Books, 1970. 143 pp.

Lists 1,423 titles published between 1724 and 1969, most of which are monographs.

Peru

159. *Anuario bibliografíco peruano.* Lima: Ediciones de la Biblioteca Nacional, 1943–.

Probably the best and most extensive of the current national bibliographies of Spanish America. Some volumes cover more than one year. Besides a classified arrangement of books published in Peru during the years covered, extensive bibliographies are published of writers who died during the period covered. It is well indexed and has a variety of special features such as a listing of periodicals published in Peru with full bibliographic details.

160. Vargas Ugarte, Rubén. *Biblioteca peruana.* Buenos Aires: Baiello, 1935–57. 12 vols.

Broad coverage of manuscripts and printed books from the colonial period.

Puerto Rico

161. *Anuario bibliográfico puertorriqueño: Indice alfabético de libros, folletos, revistas y periódicos publicados en Puerto Rico.* Río Piedras: Biblioteca de la Universidad, 1948–. Published irregularly.

Alphabetical author listing. Also contains index of publishers and book dealers.

162. Bravo, Enrique R., comp. *An Annotated Selected Puerto Rican Bibliography; Bibliografía puertorriqueña selecta anotada.* New York: Urban Center of Columbia University, 1972. 115 pp. (Spanish section) + 114 pp. (English section).

The English section is a translation of the Spanish one. Besides literature and linguistics, this book includes works on anthropology and sociology, politics, economics, education, culture, and reference works. Despite the title, many works mentioned are not annotated, and many annotations do not give a clear idea of the books' contents.

163. Pedriera, Antonio Salvador. *Bibliografía puertorriqueña (1493–1930).* Madrid: Hernando, 1932. xxxii + 707 pp.

Includes some 10,000 titles on Puerto Rico or by Puerto Ricans of all professions.

Uruguay

164. *Anuario bibliográfico uruguayo.* Montevideo: Biblioteca Nacional, 1947–.

Arrangement of books is by general Library of Congress classification. The section on periodical publications is arranged alphabetically and by subject. Contains author and publishers indexes.

165. *Bibliografía uruguaya.* Montevideo: Biblioteca del Poder Legislativo, 1962–.

Covers all publications except periodicals. Gives addresses of publishers.

166. Englekirk, John Eugene, and Margaret M. Ramos. *La narrativa uruguaya; estudio crítico-bibliográfico.* Berkeley and Los Angeles: University of California Press, 1967. 388 pp.

Part 1 is a survey of Uruguayan prose. Part 2 includes more than 400 writers and their works. Part 3 has bibliographical and author indexes.

167. Musso Ambrosi, Luis Alberto. *Bibliografía de bibliografías uruguayas, con aportes a la historia del periodismo en el Uruguay.* Montevideo: Agrupación Bibliotecológica, 1964. 102 pp.

Contains 637 entries on literature and other fields, including bibliographies from periodicals and newspapers.

168. Rela, Walter. *Fuentes para el estudio de la literatura uruguaya,*

1835–1962. Montevideo: Editores de la Banda Oriental, 1969. 134 pp.

A comprehensive bibliographic guide that updates the previous entry. Contains 900 references to books, pamphlets, and journal articles, with bibliographies, histories of literature, biographies, criticism, and anthologies. Not annotated.

Venezuela

169. *Anuario bibliográfico venezolano.* Caracas: Americana, 1942–46, 1947–54. Published in 3 vols., 1950–60.

Books and pamphlets by Venezuelan writers, Venezuelan periodicals, indexes of publishers, and author-subject-title index.

170. Carrera, Gustavo Luis. *Bibliografía de la novela venezolana.* Caracas: Universidad Central de Venezuela, Centro de Estudios Literarios, 1963. 69 pp.

Alphabetical listing of 187 novelists of the nineteenth and twentieth centuries.

171. Villasana, Angel Raúl. *Ensayo de un repertorio bibliográfico venezolano, años 1808–1950.* Caracas: Banco Central de Venezuela, 1969. 2 vols.

Annotated bibliography for years 1808–1950 of books and pamphlets; stresses authors and not subjects. Covers only ''A'' to ''CH.'' Many descriptive notes.

172. Waxman, Samuel M. *A Bibliography of the Belles-Lettres of Venezuela.* Cambridge, Mass.: Harvard University Press, 1935. xii + 145 pp.

Lists bibliographies, collections, critical works, and periodicals.

5   Literary Dictionaries and Encyclopedias

Spain and Spanish America

173. Bleiberg, Germán, and Julián Marías, eds. *Diccionario de la literatura española.* 4th ed. Madrid: Revista de Occidente, 1972 (1949). 1,261 pp.

Excellent work dealing with Spanish and Spanish American writers. Also has articles on such topics as literary terms, genres, and movements. Articles are written by well-known specialists in literature and language. Title index and also chronology of historical-political events synchronized with the evolution of letters, arts, and science.

174. *Dizionario letterario Bompiani delle opere e dei personaggi di tutti i tempi e di tutte le letterature.* Milan: Bompiani, 1947–50. 9 vols.

A dictionary that lists and describes the works of all times and all countries in literature, art, and music, with emphasis on literature.

175. *Dizionario universale delle letteratura contemporanea.* Milan: Mondadori, 1959–63. 5 vols.

Encyclopedia of world literature covering 1870–1960 and supplementing *Bompiani* (see no. 174). Includes authors, literary movements, periodicals, national literatures, and the like.

176. Newmark, Maxim. *Dictionary of Spanish Literature.* Reprint. New York: Philosophical Library, 1965 (1956). vii + 352 pp.

Limited to those names and topics usually represented in standard textbooks and outlines of Spanish and Spanish American literature. Should be used with care.

177. Sáinz de Robles, Federico. *Ensayo de un diccionario de la literatura.* Madrid: Aguilar, 1953–56. 3 vols.

Volume 1 covers literary terms, concepts, and "isms"; volume 2, Spanish and Spanish American writers; and the final volume, foreign writers. Much of his literary judgment should be taken with a grain of salt.

Spanish America [alphabetized by country or region]

Argentina

178. Becco, H. J., R. F. Giusti, A. Correia Pacheco, A. A. Roggiano, and others. *Diccionario de la literatura latinoamericana: Argentina.* Washington, D.C.: Pan American Union, 1960–61. 2 vols. (See no. 182 for format.)

179. Orgambide, Pedro G., and Roberto Yahni. *Enciclopedia de la literatura argentina.* Buenos Aires: Sudamericana, 1970. 639 pp.

An alphabetical listing of Argentine writers, works, movements, and literary genres that provides usually brief biobibliographic material and some critical studies.

180. Prieto, Adolfo. *Diccionario básico de literatura argentina.* Buenos Aires: Centro Editor de América Latina, 1968. 160 pp.

Contains brief biobibliographic sketches of Argentine writers born no later than 1930, as well as discussions of important works, literary movements, and tendencies or groups that have been significant in the development of Argentine letters.

Bolivia

181. Guzmán, Augusto. *Diccionario de la literatura latinoamericana: Bolivia.* Washington, D.C.: Pan American Union, 1957. ix + 121 pp. (See no. 182 for format.)

Central America

182. Hebblethwaite, Frank P. *Diccionario de la literatura latinoamericana: América Central.* 2d ed. Washington, D.C.: Pan American Union, 1963 (1951). Vol. 1, 136 pp.; vol. 2, 154 pp.

Volume 1—Costa Rica, El Salvador, and Guatemala; volume 2—Honduras, Nicaragua, and Panama. Each volume in this series follows a similar format. Data on each author include biographical sketches and a bibliography of the author's works and of material about him and his works.

Chile

183. Silva Castro, Raúl. *Diccionario de la literatura latinoamericana: Chile.* Washington, D.C.: Pan American Union, 1958. ix + 234 pp. (See no. 182 for format.)

Colombia

184. García Prada, Carlos. *Diccionario de la literatura latinoamericana: Colombia.* Washington, D.C.: Pan American Union, 1959. ix + 179 pp. (See no. 182 for format.)

Ecuador

185. Barrera, Isaac J., and Alejandro Carrión. *Diccionario de la literatura latinoamericana: Ecuador.* Washington, D.C.: Pan American Union, 1962. xi + 172 pp. (See no. 182 for format.)

Mexico

186. Ocampo de Gómez, Aurora, and Ernesto Prado Velázquez. *Diccionario de escritores mexicanos.* Mexico: Universidad Nacional Autónoma de México, 1967. xxviii + 422 + xlvii pp.

Biobibliographic dictionary which deals with about 500 authors.

Peru

187. Arriola Grande, F. Maurilio. *Diccionario literario del Perú; nomenclatura por autores.* Barcelona: Comercial y Artes Gráficas, 1968. 546 pp.

Biographical sketches of Peruvian authors and authors who have resided in Peru, deceased and living.

188. Romero de Valle, Emilia. *Diccionario manual de literatura peruana y materia afines.* Lima: Universidad Nacional Mayor de San Marcos, Departamento de Publicaciones, 1966. 356 pp.

Guide to past and contemporary Peruvian authors and their works. Alphabetical arrangement by author or subject. Some attention to literary genres, periodicals, and so forth.

Puerto Rico

189. Rivera de Alvarez, Josefina. *Diccionario de literatura puertorriqueña.* 3d ed. Río Piedras: Universidad de Puerto Rico, 1955 (1949). xviii + 499 pp.

Alphabetical listing of writers and their works together with a history of Puerto Rican literature and a general bibliography (pp. 155–61).

6 Histories of Hispanic Literatures

190. Cejador y Frauca, Julio. *Historia de la lengua y literatura castellana, comprendidos los autores hispano-americanos.* Madrid: Revista de Archivos, Bibliotecas y Museos, 1915–22. 14 vols. New printing, Madrid: Gredos, 1973. 7 vols.

Detailed account from origins to 1920. Bibliographies are arranged chronologically.

191. Díaz-Plaja, Guillermo, ed. *Historia general de las literaturas hispánicas.* Barcelona: Vergara, 1949–68. 7 vols.

From the earliest times to the contemporary period. Contains chapters devoted to the literature of Spanish America, the Philippines, and Spain including Castilian, Basque, Catalonian, and Galician. The work was written by a large number of contributors. The introduction by Menéndez Pidal is of particular interest. Extensive bibliographies for most chapters.

192. Díaz-Plaja, Guillermo, and Francisco Monterde. *Historia de la literatura española e historia de la literatura mexicana.* Mexico: Porrúa, 1955. 384 pp.

Concise and useful overview.

193. Díez-Echarri, Emiliano, and José María Roca Franquesa. *Historia general de la literatura española e hispanoamericana.* 2d ed. Madrid: Aguilar, 1966 (1960). xxxvi + 1,590 pp.

From the Middle Ages to the present. General bibliography as well as specific bibliographies for each section.

194. Ford, Jeremiah D. M. *Main Currents of Spanish Literature.* 2d ed. New York: Holt, 1931 (1919). vii + 284 pp.

Covers important aspects of Spanish and Spanish American literature. A series of lectures by a highly respected American Hispanist.

7   Histories of Spanish Literature

General

195. Alborg, Juan Luis. *Historia de la literatura española.* Madrid: Gredos, 1966–. 5 vols. projected.

To date three large volumes have appeared. These cover the Middle Ages and the Renaissance (see no. 212), the seventeenth century (see no. 218), and the eighteenth century (see no. 224). Extensive bibliographic information in footnotes. Alborg's ample studies of writers, periods, and genres utilize many recent scholarly contributions.

196. Amador de los Ríos, José. *Historia crítica de la literatura española.* Reprint. Madrid: Imprenta de José Rodríguez, 1942 (1861–65). 7 vols.

Extensive coverage of Roman, Visigothic, and Moorish periods. Final volume goes only to the poetry preceding the reign of Charles I.

197. Bell, Aubrey F. G. *Castilian Literature.* Oxford: Clarendon Press, 1938. xiv + 261 pp.

From *El Cid* to 1936. Bell aims to demonstrate fundamental characteristics of Castilian literature.

198. Brenan, Gerald. *The Literature of the Spanish People from Roman Times to the Present Day.* 2d ed. Cambridge: At the University Press, 1953 (1951). xvii + 496 pp.

A very subjective treatment. Brenan's value judgments are sometimes controversial but always of interest. This book omits much that the author considers inferior.

Cejador y Frauca. *Historia de la lengua y literatura castellana.* See no. 190.

199. Chandler, Richard E., and Kessel Schwartz. *A New History of Spanish Literature.* Baton Rouge: Louisiana State University Press, 1961. 696 pp.

Spanish literature arranged by genres. Extensive bibliography. Appendixes on first things in Spanish literature, common places of Spanish literature, and general historical chronology. Index of authors and titles.

200. Del Río, Angel. *Historia de la literatura española.* 2d ed. New York: Holt, Rinehart & Winston, 1963 (1948). 2 vols.

Excellent work of synthesis. Reveals a familiarity with a wide range of scholarship. Contains a bibliography at the end of each chapter, an index which includes a glossary of literary terms, and appendixes providing brief surveys of Galician and Catalonian literatures.

Díaz-Plaja. *Historia general de las literaturas hispánicas.* See no. 191.

Díez-Echarri and Roca Franquesa. *Historia general de la literatura española e hispanoamericana.* See no. 193.

201. Fitzmaurice-Kelly, James. *A History of Spanish Literature.* Rev. ed. New York: G. E. Stechert, 1926 (1898). xvi + 551 pp. Reprint, New York: Russell & Russell, 1968.

From early Spanish verse to the beginning of the twentieth century.

Ford. *Main Currents of Spanish Literature.* See no. 194.

202. García López, José. *Historia de la literatura española.* 12th ed. Barcelona:Vicens-Vives, 1968 (1948). 708 pp.

Probably the best one-volume history of Spanish literature. Contains concise but thorough treatment of periods and authors. Well-organized sections on authors include biographies and cogent analyses of their works. Bibliographies, at ends of chapters, are brief but current.

203. González López, Emilio. *Historia de la literatura española.* New York: Las Americas, 1962–65. 2 vols.

From the Middle Ages to 1900. Adequate bibliography for each chapter. Very clear, well-organized presentation.

204. Hurtado y Jiménez de la Serna, Juan, and Angel González Palencia. *Historia de la literatura española.* 6th ed. Madrid: Seata, 1949 (1921). 1,102 pp.

Extensive bibliographic material, much of which is rarely found in other manuals of literature.

205. *A Literary History of Spain.* London: Ernest Benn; and New York: Barnes & Noble, 1971–72. 6 vols. Vol. 1, *The Middle Ages* (1972), by A. D. Deyermond, 244 pp. (See no. 214.) Vol. 2, *The Golden Age: Prose and Poetry—The 16th and 17th Centuries* (1971), by R. O. Jones, 233 pp. (See no. 220.)Vol. 3, *The Golden Age: Drama, 1492–1700* (1971), by Edward M. Wilson and Duncan Moir, 171 pp. (See no. 283.) Vol. 4, *The Eighteenth Century* (1972) by Nigel Glendinning, 160 pp. (See no. 227.) Vol. 5, *The Nine-*

teenth Century (1972), by Donald L. Shaw, 200 pp. (See no. 228.) Vol. 6, *The Twentieth Century* (1972), by G. G. Brown, 176 pp. (See no. 232.)

206. Marín, Diego, and Angel del Río. *Breve historia de la literatura española.* New York: Holt, Rinehart & Winston, 1966. xvii + 394 pp. (See no. 200.)

An introductory manual based on the longer history of Del Río. From the Middle Ages to the present. Essential bibliographic information together with an index-glossary with definitions of literary terms.

207. Mérimée, Ernest. *A History of Spanish Literature (Précis d'histoire de la littérature espagnole).* Translated by S. Griswold Morley. New York: Holt, 1930 (1st French ed., 1908). xv + 635 pp.

Morley revised and enlarged the original French version. Lengthy bibliography. A well-known and often cited history.

208. Northup, George T., and Nicholson B. Adams. *An Introduction to Spanish Literature.* 3d rev. ed. Chicago: University of Chicago Press, 1960 (1925). xi + 473 pp.

An easy-to-read outline of Spanish literature.

209. Romera Navarro, Miguel. *Historia de la literatura española.* 2d ed. New York: D. C. Heath & Co., 1948 (1928). xvii + 701 pp.

From Iberians and Celts to the twentieth century. Good background information on historical, political, and artistic developments. More than usual emphasis on plot summaries and includes many passages from works studied.

210. Ticknor, George. *History of Spanish Literature.* 6th ed. Boston: Houghton Mifflin Co., 1891 (1849). 3 vols.

A classic study that is still valuable.

211. Valbuena Prat, Angel. *Historia de la literatura española.* 8th ed. Barcelona: Gustavo Gili, 1968 (1937). 4 vols. Vol. 5, *Literatura hispanoamericana,* by Angel Valbuena Briones. 4th ed., 1973 (1963).

This extensive history allows for the inclusion of less important works and writers. Frequent quotation from the literary texts analyzed. Bibliography is provided in footnotes.

Period

Medieval

212. Alborg, Juan Luis. *Historia de la literatura española.* Vol. 1, *Edad media y renacimiento.* 2d ed., 1970. 1,082 pp. (See no. 195.)
Covers Spanish literature from the Middle Ages through the sixteenth century. A preliminary chapter deals with the general characteristics and periods of Spanish literature. Alborg includes such topics as the *mester de juglaría,* the *mester de clerecía,* Alfonso X, Juan Ruiz, characteristics of the Spanish Renaissance, the theater before Lope de Vega, *Lazarillo de Tormes* and the genesis of the picaresque novel, the mystics, and didactic writers. Index of authors and works.

213. Barja, César. *Libros y autores clásicos.* Reprint. New York: G. E. Stechert, 1941 (1922). xii + 557 pp.
Covers both the Middle Ages and the Golden Age, with more space given to the latter period. Studies important writers in depth. Bibliographies.

214. Deyermond, A. D. *The Middle Ages.* Vol. 1 of *A Literary History of Spain.* New York: Barnes & Noble, 1972. 244 pp.
Begins with the earliest lyric poetry and studies the epic, the ballad, the novel, didactic literature, the *cancionero,* and liturgic drama. The *Cid* and the *Celestina* are among the important works analyzed.

215. Green, Otis H. *Spain and the Western Tradition: The Castilian Mind in Literature from* El Cid *to Calderón.* Madison: University of Wisconsin Press, 1963–66. 4 vols. Spanish translation, *España y la tradición occidental* (Madrid: Gredos, 1969. 4 vols.).
Green interprets the essential ideas of Spanish literary texts from the twelfth to the seventeenth century. Among the topics treated are love, reason, free will, fortune and fate, death, and religion. Good bibliography and useful index for each volume, and an extensive cumulative index at the end of volume 4.

216. López Estrada, Francisco. *Introducción a la literatura medieval española.* 3d ed. Madrid: Gredos, 1966 (1952). 342 pp.
Covers all aspects of medieval Spanish literature and language.

217. Millares Carlo, Agustín. *Literatura española hasta fines del siglo XV.* Mexico: Antigua Librería Robredo, 1950. 352 pp.

Includes a lengthy bibliography at the end of each chapter. The author makes use of many studies in this student manual.

Renaissance and Golden Age

218. Alborg, Juan Luis. *Historia de la literatura española.* Vol. 2, *Epoca barroca.* 2d ed., 1970. 996 pp. (See no. 195.)

Covers the seventeenth century. After a general introduction to the baroque period, Alborg treats such topics as Cervantes (170 pages), the theater from Lope de Vega to Calderón, Góngora and *culteranismo,* Quevedo and *conceptismo,* the picaresque novel, Gracián and other didactic prose writers. Index of authors and works.

Barja. *Libros y autores clásicos.* See no. 213.

219. Bell, Aubrey F. G. *El renacimiento español.* Translated by E. Juliá. Zaragoza: Ebro, 1944. xxviii + 402 pp.

A clear, sound historical and literary introduction to the period. Bibliography.

Green. *Spain and the Western Tradition.* See no. 215.

220. Jones, R. O. *The Golden Age: Prose and Poetry—The 16th and 17th Centuries.* Vol. 2 of *A Literary History of Spain.* New York: Barnes & Noble, 1971. 233 pp.

Covers the humanism of the Valdés brothers and Guevara, Garcilaso's poetry, the chivalresque, pastoral and picaresque novels, *conceptismo* and *culteranismo,* and such important writers as Cervantes, Góngora, Lope, Quevedo, and Gracián.

221. Montolíu y de Togores, Manuel de. *El alma de España y sus reflejos en la literatura del Siglo de Oro.* Barcelona: Cervantes, 1942. 752 pp.

Interrelates Spanish history, spirit, and literature.

222. Pfandl, Ludwig. *Historia de la literatura nacional española en la Edad de Oro.* Translated by Jorge Rubió Balaguer. Reprint. Barcelona: Gustavo Gili, 1952 (original German ed., 1924). 740 pp.

A classic scholarly study of the period from 1550 to 1700. Lengthy bibliographies on authors and subjects.

223. Vossler, Karl. *Introducción a la literatura española del Siglo de Oro: Seis lecciones.* Translated by Felipe González Vicén. 3d Spanish ed. Mexico: Espasa-Calpe, 1961 (1934). 151 pp.

Emphasis on the Spaniards' spiritual attitudes as revealed in their literature and language.

Eighteenth and Nineteenth Centuries

224. Alborg, Juan Luis. *Historia de la literatura española.* Vol. 3, *Siglo XVIII.* Madrid: Gredos, 1972. 979 pp.

Deals with the cultural and literary institutions and contains detailed studies of eighteenth-century writers in all genres, including such areas as erudition, history, and criticism.

225. Barja, César. *Libros y autores modernos.* Reprint. New York: Las Americas, 1964 (1924). xxvi + 466 pp.

Perceptive, detailed analyses of works by major authors of the eighteenth and nineteenth centuries. Bibliography.

226. Blanco García, P. Francisco. *La literatura española en el siglo XIX.* 3d ed. Madrid: Sáenz de Jubera, 1909–12 (1891–94). 3 vols.

Extensive treatment, including minor figures. Volume 3 deals with regional literature of Spain and Spanish America.

227. Glendinning, Nigel. *The Eighteenth Century.* Vol. 4 of *A Literary History of Spain.* New York: Barnes & Noble, 1972. 160 pp.

A reevaluation of the prose, poetry, and theater of the eighteenth century. Among the authors studied are Jovellanos, Cadalso, Meléndez Valdés, and Nicolás and Leandro Fernández de Moratín.

228. Shaw, Donald L. *The Nineteenth Century.* Vol. 5 of *A Literary History of Spain.* New York: Barnes & Noble, 1972. 200 pp.

Deals with romanticism, bourgeois high drama, the poetry of Bécquer and Rosalía de Castro, *costumbrismo, modernismo,* and the Generation of 1898.

229. Warren, L. A. *Modern Spanish Literature: A Comprehensive Survey of the Novelists, Poets, Dramatists, and Essayists from the Eighteenth Century to the Present Day.* London: Brentano's, 1929. 2 vols.

Also includes Portuguese and other authors of the Iberian Peninsula. Stresses cultural and literary characteristics of the various provinces.

Twentieth Century

230. Barja, César. *Libros y autores contemporáneos.* Reprint. New York: G. E. Stechert, 1935 (1925). 313 pp.

Studies major writers at the turn of the century: Ganivet, Unamuno, Ortega, Azorín, Baroja, Valle-Inclán, A. Machado, and Pérez de Ayala.

231. Bell, Aubrey, F. G. *Contemporary Spanish Literature*. Reprint of 3d ed. London: Russell & Russell, 1966 (1925). 313 pp.

Covers literature of second half of the nineteenth century and early part of the twentieth.

232. Brown, G. G. *The Twentieth Century*. Vol. 6 of *A Literary History of Spain*. New York: Barnes & Noble, 1972. 176 pp.

Studies the novel and poetry against the social and political events. Authors included are Unamuno, Valle-Inclán, Baroja, A. Machado, Lorca, Guillén, Jiménez, Alberti, and Cernuda.

233. Chabás, Juan. *Literatura española contemporánea, 1898–1950*. Havana: Cultural, 1952. 702 pp.

Comprehensive coverage of the first half of the twentieth century. Separate chapters are dedicated to major figures in all genres.

234. Lázaro Carreter, Fernando, and E. Correa Calderón. *Literatura española contemporánea*. 2d ed. Salamanca: Anaya, 1964 (1963). 348 pp.

An introductory manual which also includes a view of Catalan, Galician, Basque, and Spanish American literatures. Contains a short bibliography at the end of each chapter and a general bibliography at the end of the book. Author and subject indexes.

235. Madariaga, Salvador de. *De Galdós a Lorca*. Buenos Aires: Sudamericana, 1960 (1923). 223 pp. Expanded version of *The Genius of Spain and Other Essays on Spanish Contemporary Literature* (Oxford: Clarendon Press, 1923).

Suggestive essays on 11 authors. Among the authors included are Baroja, Azorín, Pérez de Ayala, Miró, and Unamuno.

236. Salinas, Pedro. *Literatura española: Siglo XX*. Reprint. Madrid: Alianza Editorial, 1970 (1941). 225 pp.

Valuable collection of essays on various authors and general themes. The comments on modernism and the Generation of 1898 are of special interest.

237. Torre, Guillermo de. *La aventura estética de nuestra edad y otros ensayos*. Barcelona: Seix Barral, 1962. 350 pp.

Analyzes the essence of literature as well as various Spanish and other European figures of the twentieth century.

238. Torrente Ballester, Gonzalo. *Literatura española contemporánea (1898–1936)*. Madrid: Afrodisio Aguado, 1949. 464 pp.

Studies ideas and themes of twentieth-century literature. Critical examination of movements and representative authors.

239. ———. *Panorama de la literatura española contemporánea*. 2d ed. Madrid: Guadarrama, 1961 (1956). 2 vols.

Volume 1 is a historical and critical study, and volume 2 is an anthology primarily devoted to the twentieth century. Volume 1 treats many writers of the previous century. There is an extremely useful bibliography of some 165 pages by J. Campos in volume 2.

Genres

Novel

240. Alborg, Juan Luis. *Hora actual de la novela española.* Madrid: Taurus, 1958–62. 2 vols.

General introduction to the Spanish novel and also contains studies devoted to 29 contemporary novelists.

241. Avalle Arce, Juan. *La novela pastoril española.* Madrid: Revista de Occidente, 1959. 248 pp.

Surveys critical studies devoted to the pastoral novel and presents the author's own analysis of this genre.

242. Balseiro, José A. *Novelistas españoles modernos.* Reprint. New York: Macmillan Co., 1947 (1933). xx + 476 pp.

Detailed studies of the major works of realists and naturalists of the nineteenth century. Includes such authors as Valera, Pereda, Galdós, and Pardo Bazán.

243. Bosch, Rafael. *La novela española del siglo XX.* New York: Las Americas, 1970–71. 2 vols.

Volume 1 deals with the generations of 1898 and 1914, and volume 2 with the generations of 1930 and 1960. Uses political, social, and historical matters to study the development of the novel with a view to showing how it contributed to the progress of contemporary life. Index of names in volume 2.

244. Chandler, Frank Wadleigh. *Romances of Roguery: The Picaresque Novel in Spain.* Reprint. New York: Burt Franklin Reprints, 1961 (1899). 483 pp.

The picaresque novel in Spain and the social and literary reasons behind its development. Also concerned with translations of picaresque novels and their incorporation into other literatures.

245. Dendel, Brian John. *The Spanish Novel of Religious Thesis, 1876–1936.* Princeton, N.J.: Princeton University, Department of Romance Languages; Madrid: Castalia, 1968. 169 pp.

Mainly discusses the historical and religious problems found in the novels of such writers as Galdós, Alarcón, Pereda, Blasco Ibáñez, Baroja, and Miró.

246. Eoff, Sherman H. *The Modern Spanish Novel: Comparative Essays Examining the Philosophical Impact of Science on Fiction.* New York: New York University Press, 1961. 280 pp. Spanish version, *El pensamiento moderno y la novela española* (Barcelona: Seix Barral, 1965).

Studies Spanish and other European novelists of the nineteenth and twentieth centuries in light of their common intellectual background. Analyzes such authors as Pereda and Dickens; Flaubert and Alas; Pardo Bazán, Galdós, and Zola; Blasco Ibáñez, Baroja, and Gorky; Unamuno; and Sender and Sartre.

247. Gil Casado, Pablo. *La novela social española (1942–1968).* Barcelona: Seix Barral, 1969. xxxviii + 335 pp.

A consideration of social realism interpreted as a continuation of the social novel of the 1930s that was influenced by Brecht and Lukacs. Takes the view that novels which began with a treatment of social problems now reveal national consciousness.

248. Gómez de Baquero, Eduardo. *El renacimiento de la novela en el siglo XIX.* Madrid: Mundo Latino, 1924. 274 pp.

The Spanish novel of the nineteenth century from the *costumbristas* to the Generation of 1898.

249. Marra-López, José R. *Narrativa española fuera de España: 1939–1961.* Madrid: Guadarrama, 1963. 539 pp.

Studies the contemporary Spanish authors living outside of Spain, such as Francisco Ayala, Max Aub, Rosa Chacel, Segundo Serrano Poncela, and Arturo Barea. Selected bibliography at the end of each chapter.

250. Menéndez Pelayo, Marcelino. *Orígenes de la novela.* Reprint. Buenos Aires: Espasa-Calpe, 1946 (1905). 3 vols. Also published as vols. 13–16 of the Edición Nacional of his *Obras completas* (Madrid: Consejo Superior de Investigaciones Científicas, 1962).

An extensive study of the novel in Spain. Treats the classical influence and the cycles of the chivalric, sentimental, historical, and pastoral novels; novels of the fifteenth and sixteenth centuries; dialogued novels; and imitations of *La Celestina* and Apuleius's *Golden Ass.* Footnotes but no bibliography.

251. Montesinos, José F. *Introducción a una historia de la novela en España en el siglo XIX, seguida del esbozo de una bibliografía de traducciones de novelas (1800–1850).* 2d ed. Madrid: Castalia, 1966 (1955). 312 pp.

A useful introduction to the development of the nineteenth-century Spanish novel.

252. Parker, Alexander A. *Literature and the Delinquent: The Picaresque Novel in Spain and Europe, 1599–1753*. Edinburgh: University Press, 1967. 195 pp. Spanish version, *Los pícaros en la literatura: La novela picaresca en España y Europa, 1599–1753* (Madrid: Gredos, 1971).

Assesses the value of certain Spanish and German novels in the period before Defoe and Lesage. It is not a complete survey but offers new insights into the history of the genre.

253. Pérez Minik, Domingo. *Novelistas españoles de los siglos XIX y XX*. Madrid: Guadarrama, 1957. 352 pp.

Studies many authors of the modern period but also includes studies of the picaresque novels of Mateo Alemán and Quevedo.

254. Rennert, Hugo A. *The Spanish Pastoral Romances*. New York: Biblo & Tannen, 1968 (1892). 206 pp. Reprint of the 1912 rev. ed.

A brief review of 22 pastoral romances that appeared in Spain for nearly a century after the publication of Montemayor's *Diana* (ca. 1559).

255. Sáinz de Robles, Federico. *La novela española en el siglo XX*. Madrid: Pegaso, 1957. 302 pp.

Mainly biobibliographic material on twentieth-century novelists. Includes a general as well as an author bibliography.

256. Siles Artés, José. *El arte de la novela pastoril*. Valencia: Albatros, 1972. 172 pp.

The evolution of the Spanish pastoral novel with most emphasis on Montemayor's *Diana*. Bibliography.

257. Sobejano, Gonzalo. *Novela española de nuestro tiempo (en busca del pueblo perdido)*. Madrid: Prensa Española, 1970. 479 pp.

Studies the return of the Spanish novel to realism after the Civil War. Among the selected novelists examined are: Cela, Laforet, and Delibes, writers who illustrate existential realism; and Sánchez Ferlosio, Fernández Santos, and Juan Goytisolo, novelists who are social realists.

258. Zamora Vicente, Alonso. *¿Qué es la novela picaresca?* Buenos Aires: Columba, 1962. 69 pp.

Concise introduction to this genre, with plot summaries.

Theater

259. Aubrun, Charles V. *La comedia española (1600–1680)*. Translation of *La comédie espagnole (1600–1680)*. Madrid: Taurus, 1968 (1966). 320 pp.

Social, historical background is presented along with studies of individual dramatists of the Golden Age.

260. Borel, Jean Paul. *El teatro de lo imposible: Ensayo sobre una de las dimensiones fundamentales del teatro español contemporáneo.* Translated from the French by G. Torrente Ballester. 2d Spanish ed. Madrid: Guadarrama, 1966 (1963). 304 pp.

Descriptive-critical study of the feeling of frustration (the unattainable) in the contemporary Spanish theater through the works of its most established dramatists.

261. Campos, Jorge. *Teatro y sociedad de España (1780–1820).* Madrid: Editorial Moneda y Crédito, 1969. 215 pp.

Studies the Spanish theater in the period between neoclassicism and romanticism. Bibliographic footnotes.

262. Cook, John A. *Neo-Classic Drama in Spain: Theory and Practice.* Dallas, Tex.: Southern Methodist University Press, 1959. 567 pp.

Detailed and well-documented analysis of neoclassic drama from the time of Luzán's *Poetics* through the failures of romanticism. Contains general and play indexes.

263. Crawford, James P. W. *Spanish Drama before Lope de Vega.* Reprint. Philadelphia: University of Pennsylvania Press, 1967 (1922). 211 pp.

Traces the development of drama from pre-Encina times to the religious drama and the tragedy and comedy of the late sixteenth century. This is a reprint of the 1937 edition together with a new bibliographic supplement by W. T. MacCready.

264. ———. *The Spanish Pastoral Drama.* Philadelphia: University of Pennsylvania Press, 1915. 126 pp.

Pastoral plays from the period before Juan del Encina until the seventeenth century, including those by Lope de Vega and Calderón.

265. Díaz de Escobar, Narciso, and Francisco P. Lasso de la Vega. *Historia del teatro español: Comediantes, escritores, curiosidades escénicas.* Barcelona: Montaner y Simón, 1924. 2 vols.

In addition, this study includes J. Bernat Durán's examination of the theater of Catalonia and Valencia.

266. Donovan, Richard B. *Liturgical Drama in Medieval Spain.* Toronto: Pontifical Institute of Medieval Studies, 1948. 229 pp.

Studies the liturgical drama in Spain and its possible relationship with the development of Spanish medieval drama and the liturgical drama of France. It presents for the first time texts uncovered by the author, primarily in Catalonia. Bibliography and detailed index of the new texts.

267. Guerrero Zamora, Juan. *Historia del teatro contemporáneo.* Barcelona: Juan Flors, 1967. 4 vols.

Extensive treatment of contemporary playwrights of Spain and the world, taking into account not only the literary aspects of theater but also the importance of scenario and of contemporary thought. Discusses such writers as Lorca, Valle-Inclán, Galdós, and Echegaray.

268. Hermenegildo, Alfredo. *Los trágicos españoles del siglo XVI.* Madrid: Fundación Universitaria Española, 1961. 617 pp.

Reevaluation of previous criticism and presentation of new insights into Spanish tragedy. Bibliography of and about each author as well as an appendix of characters, plots, and verse forms of the many tragedies studied in the text.

269. Lázaro Carreter, Fernando. *Teatro medieval.* 2d ed. Valencia: Castalia, 1965 (1958). 285 pp.

From the *Auto de los Reyes Magos* to Comendador Escrivá. Excellent introduction to the medieval theater together with an anthology.

270. Leavitt, Sturgis E. *Golden Age Drama in Spain: General Considerations and Unusual Features.* Chapel Hill: University of North Carolina Press, 1972. 128 pp.

Seventeen essays that emphasize the role of the public in shaping the Spanish *comedia*. The first two essays are general.

271. López Morales, Humberto. *Tradición y creación en los orígenes del teatro castellano.* Madrid: Alcalá, 1968. 259 pp.

A study of the medieval tradition found in the early sixteenth-century theater and of the attempts to introduce changes. The author finds it difficult to defend the existence of a medieval liturgical theater.

272. McClelland, I. L. *Spanish Drama of Pathos, 1750–1808.* Liverpool: University Press, 1970. 2 vols.

Major work on the drama of the Enlightenment with special reference to its European context. Treats translations, opera, parody, and experimentation in new dramatic methods.

273. Muñoz, Matilde. *Historia del teatro en España.* Madrid: Tesora, 1965. 3 vols.

Volume 1 reviews highlights of the Spanish drama and comedy, volume 2 treats the opera and the Teatro Real, and volume 3 is a history of the *zarzuela* and the *género chico*. No bibliography or index.

274. Parker, Jack Horace. *Breve historia del teatro español.* Mexico: Ediciones de Andrea, 1957. 213 pp.

General overview of the Spanish theater from the Middle Ages to the 1950s. Includes index of dramatists and *dramas anónimos* and ample bibliography.

275. Rennert, Hugo A. *The Spanish Stage in the Time of Lope de Vega.* Reprint. New York: Dover Publications, 1963 (1909). 403 pp.

Reprint of the first edition except for the omission of ''List of Spanish Actors and Actresses, 1560–1680.'' Discusses major playwrights, origins of the *comedia* and other types of plays, famous theaters, staging of plays, notable actors, and the like. A classic study of the Spanish stage.

276. Ruiz Ramón, Francisco. *Historia del teatro español.* Madrid: Alianza Editorial, 1967–71. 2 vols.

Volume 1 treats major writers from the *Auto de los Reyes Magos* to Galdós. Appendixes on the *Celestina* and the classification of the theater of major dramatists of the seventeenth century. Volume 2 covers the period from Benavente to 1968. One section deals with politically oriented plays written during the Civil War.

277. Sánchez Escribano, F., and A. Porqueras Mayo. *Preceptiva dramática española del renacimiento y el barroco.* Madrid: Gredos, 1965. 258 pp.

A useful compilation of passages on dramatic theory taken from writers of the Golden Age.

278. Shergold, N. D. *A History of the Spanish Stage from Medieval Times until the End of the Seventeenth Century.* Oxford: Clarendon Press, 1967. xxx + 624 pp.

An extensive study of the staging of theatrical productions. Numerous illustrations, glossary, and bibliography.

279. Torrente Ballester, Gonzalo. *Teatro español contemporáneo.* 2d ed. Madrid: Guadarrama, 1968 (1957). 606 pp.

Examines general themes in contemporary Spanish drama and includes a chapter on the most important authors (Lorca, Casona, Sastre, Buero). It treats such themes as *teatro de evasión,* the *soltera insatisfecha,* and Don Juan.

280. Valbuena Prat, Angel. *Historia del teatro español.* Barcelona: Noguer, 1956. 708 pp.

Stresses themes of the Spanish theater from the beginnings to the middle of this century. Contains indexes but little bibliography. Illustrations of dramatists and scenes from plays.

281. ———. *Teatro moderno español*. 2d ed. Zaragoza: Partenón, 1954 (1944). 184 pp.

Studies the principal motifs of the Spanish theater from the decline of the Golden Age to the twentieth century.

282. Wardropper, Bruce. *Introducción al teatro religioso del Siglo de Oro: Evolución del auto sacramental antes de Calderón*. 2d ed. Salamanca: Anaya, 1967 (1953). 339 pp.

Treats the development of an important Spanish dramatic form in all its aspects as well as the works of some of the authors.

283. Wilson, E. M., and Duncan Moir. *The Golden Age: Drama, 1492–1700*. Vol. 3 of *A Literary History of Spain*. New York: Barnes & Noble, 1971. 177 pp.

Begins with the *églogas* of Encina and studies the development of the drama through Rueda, Cervantes, Lope, Tirso, and Calderón.

284. Wilson, Margaret. *Spanish Drama of the Golden Age*. Oxford: Pergamon, 1969. 211 pp.

Introduction to the dramatists and the social and historical background of the Golden Age theater. Ample bibliography.

Short Story

285. Anderson-Imbert, Enrique. *El cuento español*. Buenos Aires: Columba, 1959. 47 pp.

Defines the term *cuento* and briefly relates its development in Spain from the Middle Ages to the present. The appendix is a guide to 20 significant writers of this century.

286. Baquero Goyanes, Mariano. *El cuento español en el siglo XIX*. Madrid: Consejo Superior de Investigaciones Científicas, 1949. 699 pp.

Studies the various kinds of short stories in the nineteenth century, such as historical, fantastic, humorous, and religious.

287. Bourland, Caroline Brown. *The Short Story in Spain in the Seventeenth Century*. Northampton, Mass.: Smith College, 1927. 215 pp.

Brief essay on the characteristics of the Spanish short story in the seventeenth century and the Italian influence upon it. Bibliography of editions of novels in the seventeenth and eighteenth centuries.

Essay

288. Bleznick, Donald W. *El ensayo español del siglo XVI al XX.* Mexico: Ediciones de Andrea, 1964. 140 pp.

Covers development of the essay from the sixteenth century to 1960, with most emphasis on the twentieth century. Ample bibliographies.

289. Marichal, Juan. *La voluntad de estilo.* Reprint. Madrid: Revista de Occidente, 1971 (1957). 271 pp.

Synthesizes the representative traits of Spanish essayists from Pulgar to Castro and Salinas. Points out their individuality, indicating at the same time the fitness of their styles to their historical epochs. The nineteenth century is omitted. Bibliography.

Poetry

290. Alonso, Dámaso. *Poetas españoles contemporáneos.* 3d ed. Madrid: Gredos, 1965 (1952). 424 pp.

Studies Bécquer, the Machado brothers, Salinas, Guillén, Lorca, Aleixandre, Panero, Rosales, and others.

291. Aub, Max. *Poesía española contemporánea.* Mexico: Era, 1969. 239 pp.

Survey of Spanish poetry from the Generation of 1898 to the 1950s, with emphasis on the social, economic, and political background.

292. Debicki, Andrew P. *Estudios sobre poesía española contemporánea (la generación de 1924–1925).* Madrid: Gredos, 1968. 333 pp.

A panoramic view of the attitudes and theories of this group of poets. Detailed analyses of certain aspects of the works of Salinas, Guillén, Dámaso Alonso, Lorca, Alberti, G. Diego, Cernuda, and Prados.

293. Díaz-Plaja, Guillermo. *Historia de la poesía lírica española.* 2d ed. Barcelona: Labor, 1948 (1937). 456 pp.

Comprehensive overview of lyric poetry.

294. García Gómez, Emilio. *Las jarchas romances de la serie árabe en su marco.* Madrid: Sociedad de Estudios y Publicaciones, 1965. 431 pp.

Study and anthology of 43 Andalusian *muwassahas* in Roman alphabet, and also their Spanish versions. Appendixes on Hebrew

jarchas, metrics of the *muwassahas,* and information on the authors
of these poems. Also contains glossary for the *jarchas* included in
the book.

295. Menéndez Pidal, Ramón. *La epopeya castellana a través de la
literatura española.* 1st Spanish ed. Buenos Aires: Espasa-Calpe,
1959 (1910). 245 pp.

Indispensable study. Traces the ever present influence of the epic
throughout Spanish literature from the *Cid* to modern poetry, stres-
sing the wealth of national tradition which the epic embraces.

296. ———. *Los godos y la epopeya española: Chansons de gestes y
baladas nórdicas.* Madrid: Espasa-Calpe, 1956. 255 pp.

Origins of the epic and its relation with Gothic culture. Subject
index and footnotes.

297. ———. *Poesía juglaresca y orígenes de las literaturas hispánicas.* 6th ed. Madrid: Instituto de Estudios Políticos, 1957 (1924).
488 pp.

The nature of the *juglar,* and his role and influence upon narrative
verse. More extensive than the first edition. Contains abundant footnotes, author and subject indexes, and an appendix on the *juglares* of
the courts of Sancho IV and Jaime I of Aragon.

298. ———. *El romancero español.* 2d ed. New York. Hispanic Society of America, 1928 (1910). 131 pp.

Studies the nature and evolution of the *romancero.*

299. Milá y Fontanals, Manuel. *De la poesía heroico-popular castellana.* Barcelona: Consejo Superior de Investigaciones Científicas,
1959. 623 pp.

From the epics of Rodrigo through the Carolingian and Breton
cycles. Contains a wealth of footnotes, author and subject indexes,
and a new classification of the *romances* and their themes. This is an
indispensable source.

300. Morris, C. B. *A Generation of Spanish Poets (1920–1936).*
Cambridge: At the University Press, 1969. 301 pp.

Analysis of this generation, indicating attitudes of each poet
toward the various artistic experiments and showing how each ma-
tures to gain an original style.

301. Nykl, Alois R. *Hispano-Arabic Poetry and Its Relation with
the Old Provenzal Troubadours.* Baltimore: J. H. Furst, 1946.
xxvii + 416 pp.

Author's thesis is that Islamic civilization influenced the medieval
lyricism of Moorish Spain.

302. Pierce, Frank. *La poesía épica del Siglo de Oro.* 2d ed. Madrid: Gredos, 1968 (1961). 396 pp.

A survey of criticism of past centuries and an analysis of some epic poems. Appendixes include catalogs of published epic poems, translations, and editions of the eighteenth through twentieth centuries.

303. Siebenmann, Gustav. *Los estilos poéticos en España desde 1900.* Spanish translation by Angel San Miguel. Madrid: Gredos, 1973. 582 pp.

Studies the poetry of *modernismo* and the Generation of 1898; "pure poetry," "neopopularism," surrealism, and other "isms" of "dehumanized" poetry that began around 1920; and the "rehumanized" poetry that began around 1940. Includes two extensive bibliographies: a chronological listing of books of poetry (1883–1971), and a list of books consulted.

304. Stern, S. M. *Les chansons mozarabes.* 2d ed. London: Bruno Cassirer Oxford, 1964 (1953). 63 pp.

Study of more than 40 *jarchas* of Arabic and Hebrew *muwassahas* by the discoverer of this earliest lyric poetry in Spain.

305. Vivanco, Luis Felipe. *Introducción a la poesía española contemporánea.* 2d ed. Madrid: Guadarrama, 1971 (1957). 2 vols.

Studies the poetry of Juan Ramón Jiménez, Guillén, Salinas, León Felipe, Gerardo Diego, Alberti, Cernuda, Lorca, Dámaso Alonso, Ridruejo, and others. Biobibliographic notes on each poet represented and an introduction on the meaning of lyric poetry.

306. Wardropper, Bruce. *Historia de la poesía lírica a lo divino en la cristiandad occidental.* Madrid: Revista de Occidente, 1958. 344 pp.

An examination of the poetic phenomenon of converting profane works into sacred ones.

307. Zardoya, Concha. *Poesía española contemporánea: Estudios temáticos y estilísticos.* Madrid: Guadarrama, 1961. 724 pp.

Detailed and thought-provoking study of the most distinguished modern Spanish poets: Bécquer, Unamuno, A. Machado, Salinas, Jiménez, Guillén, Lorca, Hernández, Aleixandre, and others. Bibliography and general index.

Literary Movements

See also chapter 8, pp. 78–80, for works on *modernismo*.

308. Cotarelo y Mori, Emilio. *Iriarte y su época.* Madrid: Sucesores de Rivadeneyra, 1897. 588 pp.

Despite the use of Iriarte as a focal point, this book is a history of the entire neoclassical movement in the eighteenth century.

309. Díaz-Plaja, Guillermo. *El espíritu del barroco: Tres interpretaciones.* Barcelona: Apolo, 1940. 129 pp.

Suggestive introduction to the baroque. Claims that Quevedo's *La hora de todos* is the key work of the period.

310. ———. *Introducción al estudio del romanticismo español.* 2d ed. Madrid: Espasa-Calpe, 1942 (1936). 309 pp.

Helpful in pointing out characteristics of the romantic period. General schematic overview.

311. Granjel, Luis S. *Panorama de la generación del 98.* Madrid: Guadarrama, 1959. 535 pp.

Thematic study of the writers of this generation. Presents the ideology of these writers and also provides brief selections from their writings.

312. Gullón, Ricardo. *Direcciones del modernismo.* Madrid: Gredos, 1963. 242 pp.

Describes the movement and contrasts it with other styles. Juan Ramón Jiménez and the Machado brothers are some of the specific authors to whom considerable attention is given.

313. ———. *La invención del '98 y otros ensayos.* Madrid: Gredos, 1969. 199 pp.

Studies the period of the *modernistas* and the Generation of 1898 and relates these Spanish writers to other European authors.

314. Hatzfeld, Helmut. *Estudios literarios sobre mística española.* 2d ed. Madrid: Gredos, 1968 (1955). 423 pp.

Mysticism in Spain and its relationship to other European writers and mystics.

315. ———. *Estudios sobre el barroco.* 2d ed. Madrid: Gredos, 1966 (1964). 491 pp.

This study is based on earlier published articles. Examines the baroque in Spain, Italy, France, and Portugal. Concentrates on such Spanish writers as Góngora, Gracián, Lope de Vega, and Cervantes.

316. Ilie, Paul. *The Surrealist Mode in Spanish Literature: An Interpretation of Basic Trends from Post-Romanticism to the Spanish Vanguard.* Ann Arbor: University of Michigan Press, 1968. 242 pp. Spanish version, *Los surrealistas españoles* (Madrid: Taurus, 1972). 323 pp.

A perceptive and comprehensive study of surrealism in Spanish literature.

317. Jeschke, Hans. *La generación de 1898: Ensayo de una deter-*

minación de su esencia. Translated by Y. Pino Saavedra. Madrid: Editora Nacional, 1954 (1934). 177 pp.

Traces the influences and origins of this generation. Views this group of writers as a spiritual generation.

318. **Jiménez, Juan Ramón.** *El modernismo: Notas de un curso (1953).* Mexico: Aguilar, 1962. 369 pp.

A sensitive study of *modernismo* by a major poet. Prologue and notes by Ricardo Gullón and E. Fernández Méndez. Appendixes include prologue and index to Federico de Onís's *Antología de la poesía española e hispanoamericana.*

319. **Laín Entralgo, Pedro.** *La generación del noventa y ocho.* Buenos Aires: Espasa-Calpe, 1947. 265 pp.

Perceptively analyzes the major writers of the Generation of 1898 and reveals that it was a genuine Spanish literary generation to which Laín's generation is indebted.

320. **McClelland, I. L.** *The Origins of the Romantic Movement in Spain.* Liverpool: University Press, 1937. Reprint, New York: Barnes & Noble Books, 1974.

Takes the point of view that Spanish literature is essentially romantic in nature. Follows the trend of national instinctive romanticism during the classical eighteenth century to the self-conscious romanticism of the nineteenth century.

321. **Morris, C. B.** *Surrealism and Spain, 1920–1936.* Cambridge: At the University Press, 1972. 291 pp.

Deals with French surrealist influences on Spanish writers and artists and with the themes, motifs, moods, and techniques used by Spanish and Catalan authors. Contains several appendixes of documentary materials, poems, lectures, and other writings in French, Spanish, and Catalan. Select critical bibliography.

322. **Navas-Ruiz, Ricardo.** *El romaticismo español: Historia y crítica.* Salamanca-Madrid: Anaya, 1970. 332 pp.

Studies the development of Spanish romanticism from its beginnings in the eighteenth century.

323. **Pattison, Walter T.** *El naturalismo español: Historia externa de un movimiento literario.* Madrid: Gredos, 1965. 190 pp.

Contains important writings dealing with naturalism in Spain; and critical studies, book reviews, and the like. Based primarily on periodicals published from 1875 to 1897.

324. **Peers, E. Allison.** *Historia del movimiento romántico español.* Madrid: Gredos, 1954. 2 vols. Translation by J. M. Gimeno of *A History of the Romantic Movement in Spain* (Cambridge, 1940).

Extensive data on the origins, influences, literary battles, and rise and fall of romanticism. Peers's condensed work (230 pp.) on the subject is *The Romantic Movement in Spain: A Short History* (Liverpool: University Press, 1968).

325. ———. *Studies of the Spanish Mystics.* London: Sheldon, 1927–30. 2 vols.

Extensive study from Saint Ignatius of Loyola to post-Teresan mysticism. Lengthy bibliography.

326. Piñeyro, Enrique, and E. Allison Peers (trans.). *The Romantics of Spain.* Liverpool: Institute of Hispanic Studies, 1934. 256 pp.

Biographical and critical essays on the chief and some minor writers of the romantic period. Select bibliography and index.

327. Sender, Ramón. *Examen de ingenios: Los noventayochos.* New York: Las Americas, 1961. 326 pp.

A very personal evaluation of such writers as Unamuno, Valle-Inclán, Baroja, Azorín, Maeztu, and Machado. Sender minimizes Unamuno's literary contributions.

328. Torre, Guillermo de. *Historia de las literaturas de vanguardia.* 2d ed. Madrid: Guadarrama, 1971 (1965). 3 vols.

Basic work on literary movements of the twentieth century. A survey of an extremely wide range of authors from the Italian futurists and German expressionism to concretism, the "angry young men," and the "beatniks."

329. ———. *Ultraísmo, existencialismo y objetivismo en literatura.* Madrid: Guadarrama, 1968. 320 pp.

Studies the three vanguardist movements that have most influenced Spanish and Spanish American literature from 1920 to the present.

330. Videla, Gloria. *El ultraísmo.* Madrid: Gredos, 1963. 246 pp.

Introduction to vanguardist literary movements of the twentieth century in Spain.

8   Histories of Spanish American Literature

General

331. Alegría, Fernando. *Historia de la novela hispanoamericana.* 2d ed. Mexico: Ediciones de Andrea, 1965 (1959). 301 pp.

Comprehensive coverage of the Spanish American novel that begins with Fernández de Lizardi and comes up to the 1960s. General bibliography and bibliographies for specific novelists.

332. Amorós, Andrés. *Introducción a la novela hispanoamericana actual.* Salamanca: Anaya, 1971. 181 pp.

Essays on such contemporary authors as Carpentier, Sábato, Cortázar, Rulfo, Fuentes, and García Márquez.

333. Anderson-Imbert, Enrique. *Historia de la literatura hispanoamericana.* 4th ed. Mexico: Fondo de Cultura Económica, 1962 (1954). 2 vols. English translation by John V. Falconieri, *Spanish American Literature: A History* (Detroit: Wayne State University Press, 1963). 617 pp.

Follows the generational approach in organization. A vast number of authors and works are given brief presentations.

334. Arrom, José Juan. *Esquema generacional de las letras hispanoamericanas.* Bogota: Instituto Caro y Cuervo, 1963. 241 pp.

Studies from a generational point of view. The nineteenth-century political, or regional, approach is rejected in favor of a continental and chronological one. The opening chapter is a review of the attempts to bring order out of the apparent chaos of names and dates pertaining to Spanish American literature.

335. ———. *Historia del teatro hispanoamericano (época colonial).* Mexico: Ediciones de Andrea, 1967. 151 pp. Published originally as *El teatro de Hispanoamérica en la época colonial* (Havana: Anuario Bibliográfico Cubano, 1956). 237 pp.

Valuable handbook that goes from indigenous theater to *costumbrismo.*

336. Aubrun, Charles V. *Histoire des lettres hispanoaméricaines.* Paris: Armand Colin, 1954. 224 pp.

Concise, general introduction. Bibliographies.

337. Barbagelata, Hugo D. *La novela y el cuento en Hispanoamérica.* Montevideo: Enrique Miguez, 1947. 316 pp.

Includes all Spanish-speaking countries in America. Bibliography.

338. Barrera, Isaac J. *Literatura hispanoamericana.* Quito: Universidad Central, 1934. 459 pp.

From the conquest to the modern period.

339. Bazin, Robert. *Histoire de la littérature américaine de langue espagnole.* Paris: Firmin-Didot, 1953. 354 pp.

From 1800 to the 1950s. Appendixes treat contemporary literary trends and national literature.

340. Blanco-Fombona, Rufino. *Grandes escritores de América (siglo XIX).* Madrid: Renacimiento, 1917. 343 pp.

Comments on five major writers of the nineteenth century: Bello, Sarmiento, Hostos, Montalvo, and González Prada. No bibliography.

341. Carvalho, Joaquim de Montezuma de. *Panorama das literaturas das Américas (de 1900 á actualidade).* Angola: Edição do Município de Nova Lisboa, 1958–65. 4 vols.

Collection of 35 studies by individual writers on Brazil, North America, and South America. Volume 4 has articles by Fernando Alegría on Chile, Luis Leal on Mexico, and José Ramón Medina on Venezuela.

342. Castagnaro, R. Anthony. *The Early Spanish American Novel.* New York: Las Americas, 1971. 208 pp.

From the colonial beginnings through the nineteenth century, with emphasis on nineteenth-century Mexican and Argentine novels. Also includes *indianista,* antislavery, realistic, and historical novels. Short bibliography.

Cejador y Frauca. *Historia de la lengua y literatura castellana.* See no. 190.

343. Coester, Alfred. *The Literary History of Spanish America.* 2d ed. New York: Macmillan Co., 1928 (1916). xii + 522 pp.

Emphasis is on facts and plot summaries. First literary history of Spanish America. Judgments often differ from those of today.

344. Daireaux, Max. *Panorama de la littérature hispano-américaine.* Paris: Kra, 1930. 314 pp.

From Independence to the 1920s.

345. Dauster, Frank. *Historia del teatro hispanoamericano (siglos XIX y XX).* Mexico: Ediciones de Andrea, 1966. 121 pp.

A comprehensive survey with ample bibliography.

Díaz Plaja. *Historia general de las literaturas hispánicas.* See no. 191.

346. **Díez Canedo, Enrique.** *Letras de América: Estudios sobre las literaturas continentales.* Mexico: Fondo de Cultura Económica, 1944. 426 pp.

Studies in depth of writers of the nineteenth and twentieth centuries.

Díez-Echarri and Roca Franquesa. *Historia general de la literatura española e hispanoamericana.* See no. 193.

347. **Earle, Peter G., and Robert G. Mead, Jr.** *Historia del ensayo hispanoamericano.* Mexico: Ediciones de Andrea, 1973. 173 pp. Earlier version by Mead, *Breve historia del ensayo hispanoamericano* (Mexico: Ediciones de Andrea, 1956). 144 pp.

A biobibliographic study from the colonial period to the present. Extensive bibliographies.

348. **Englekirk, John E., Irving A. Leonard, John T. Reid, and John A. Crow.** *An Outline History of Spanish American Literature.* 3d ed. New York: Appleton-Century-Crofts, 1965 (1941). xii + 252 pp.

Excellent outline history intended for students. Brief introductions to periods and authors, including bibliographies. Bibliographies on history, anthologies, literary history, and criticism.

349. **Ferro, Hellén.** *Historia de la poesía hispanoamericana.* New York: Las Americas, 1964. 428 pp.

Outline history of Spanish American poetry from colonial period to present. Not a penetrating study but contains important names and facts.

350. **Franco, Jean.** *An Introduction to Spanish American Literature.* Cambridge: At the University Press, 1969. ix + 390 pp.

Deals mainly with literature of Spanish America from time of Independence. Author attempts to cover common characteristics as well as national differences.

351. **Fuentes, Carlos.** *La nueva novela hispanoamericana.* Mexico: Joaquín Mortiz, 1969. 98 pp.

Personal study on most outstanding contemporary writers, such as Borges, Vargas Llosa, Carpentier, García Márquez, Cortázar, and Juan Goytisolo.

352. **Gallo, Ugo, and Giuseppe Bellini.** *Storia della letteratura ispano-americana.* 2d ed. Milan: Nuova Academia Editrice, 1958 (1954). 482 pp.

Divided into four parts: from colonial period to Independence, the romantic period, modernism, and the twentieth century. Extensive bibliography of anthologies and critical studies. In the attempt to cover many authors of all the Spanish American countries, most writers are given scant individual attention, especially in the last part.

353. Gertel, Zunilda. *La novela hispanoamericana contemporánea.* Buenos Aires: Columba-Nuevos Esquemas, 1970. 200 pp.

Studies the outstanding novels from the beginning of the twentieth century to the 1960s. Romanticism, realism, regionalism, modernism, and the new novel are covered.

354. Gómez-Gil, Orlando. *Historia crítica de la literatura hispanoamericana.* New York: Holt, Rinehart & Winston, 1968. xiv + 768 pp.

Studies major authors as well as secondary ones who have importance in literary developments of their period. Discussions by regions or countries are avoided. Some errors of factual information. Good bibliographies.

355. Hamilton, Carlos. *Historia de la literatura hispanoamericana.* New York: Las Americas, 1960–61. 2 vols. 2d ed., Madrid: Ediciones y Publicaciones Españolas, 1966. 397 pp.

Highlights of Spanish American literary production with background information on various periods. First part covers the colonial period and the nineteenth century, and the second includes modernism and the twentieth century.

356. Harss, Luis, and Barbara Dohmann. *Into the Mainstream: Conversations with Latin American Writers.* New York: Harper & Row, 1969. 385 pp. Spanish version, *Los nuestros,* 4th ed. (Buenos Aires: Sudamericana, 1971 [1966]). 465 pp.

Studies the literary styles of Carpentier, Asturias, Borges, Onetti, Cortázar, Fuentes, Rulfo, García Márquez, and Vargas Llosa.

357. Henríquez-Ureña, Pedro. *Literary Currents in Hispanic America.* Cambridge, Mass.: Harvard University Press, 1945. Spanish title, *Las corrientes literarias en la América hispánica,* 2d ed. (Mexico: Fondo de Cultura Económica, 1954 [1949]). 237 pp.

Introduction to the important men, ideas, and epochs of Latin American literature. Follows rigorous chronological scheme, dividing material (1492–1940) into seven stages of development. Lengthy bibliography.

358. Jones, Willis Knapp. *Behind Spanish American Footlights.* Austin: University of Texas Press, 1966. xvi + 609 pp.

Very informative study of the theater from indigenous to present. Lengthy bibliography including unpublished theses.

359. ———. *Breve historia del teatro latinoamericano*. Mexico: Ediciones de Andrea, 1956. 239 pp.

Concise study with ample bibliography.

360. Lazo, Raimundo. *Historia de la literatura hispanoamericana*. Mexico: Porrúa, 1965–67. 2 vols.

From the colonial period to 1914.

361. Leal, Luis. *Breve historia de la literatura hispanoamericana*. New York: Alfred A. Knopf, 1971. 392 pp.

Survey of Spanish American literature from pre-Columbian times to 1970. Extensive bibliographies.

362. ———. *Historia del cuento hispanoamericano*. Mexico: Ediciones de Andrea, 1966. 175 pp.

Cogent study with ample bibliography.

363. Leguizamón, Julio A. *Historia de la literatura hispanoamericana*. Buenos Aires: Editoriales Reunidas, 1945. 2 vols.

From colonial era to about 1900. Material is divided into four epochs within which the organization is according to geographical regions or literary genres. Volume 2 contains index and bibliography by country.

364. Meléndez, Concha. *La novela indianista en Hispanoamérica (1832–1889)*. Río Piedras: Universidad de Puerto Rico, 1961 (1934). 202 pp.

Treats origins of the *novela indianista* (literature of the conquest and foreign influences), historical and poetic novels, and novels with the theme of social injustices. Good bibliography.

365. Menéndez Pelayo, Marcelino. *Historia de la poesía hispanoamericana*. Reprint. Santander: Consejo Superior de Investigaciones Científicas, 1948 (1911). 2 vols.

One chapter devoted to each Spanish American country. Covers poetry up to about 1875. Index at end of each volume facilitates use of anthology compiled by same author.

366. Olivera, Otto. *Breve historia de la literatura antillana*. Mexico: Ediciones de Andrea, 1957. 222 pp.

Concise treatment of the literatures of Cuba, Dominican Republic, and Puerto Rico from the sixteenth century to the middle of the twentieth. Ample bibliography.

367. Ortega, Julio. *La contemplación y la fiesta: Ensayos sobre la novela latinoamericana*. Caracas: Monte Avila, 1969. 328 pp.

Contains a detailed analysis of language as protagonist in Lezama Lima's *Paradiso*. Also includes conquest of reality by poetry, metaphoric descriptions of speech, and initiation into poetry.

368. Pupo-Walker, Enrique, ed. *El cuento hispanoamericano ante la crítica.* Madrid: Castalia, 1973. 383 pp.

Twenty-four articles by as many critics, some of them outstanding, that study well-known *cuentistas* and the *cuento* in Mexico, Chile, Peru, and contemporary Cuba. Pupo-Walker provides a concise overview of the Spanish American *cuento*.

369. Rodríguez Monegal, Emir. *El arte de narrar.* Caracas: Monte Avila, 1968. 311 pp.

Interviews with 12 writers, all Latin Americans except for Max Aub and Juan Goytisolo. Among the others included are Homero Aridjis, Cabrera Infante, Fuentes, Sábato, and Sarduy. Brief biobibliographic introductions to each author.

370. ———. *Narradores de esta América.* Vol. 1. Montevideo: Alfa, 1968. 359 pp.

Evaluates modern novelists of Latin America: Azuela, Quiroga, Gallegos, Borges, Marechal, Mallea, and others. Introductory analysis of the new novel.

371. Rosenbaum, Sidonia Carmen. *Modern Women Poets of Spanish America.* New York: Hispanic Institute, 1945. 273 pp.

Study of women poets since the colonial period. Analyzes Delmira Agustini at length but also includes studies on Mistral, Storni, and Ibarbourou. Extensive bibliography.

372. Sánchez, Luis Alberto. *Escritores representativos de América.* 1st ser., 2d ed. Madrid: Gredos, 1963 (1957), 3 vols.; 2d ser., 1963, 3 vols.

The two series total 100 chapters (50 in each) devoted to 100 different authors from the sixteenth century to the contemporary period. Bibliography of works by and about each author.

373. ———. *Nueva historia de la literatura americana.* 2d ed. Buenos Aires: Guaranía, 1950 (1944). 598 pp.

Begins with pre-Columbian literature and ends with an appendix on the literary tendencies of post–World War I. Organization of material is chronological and thematic.

374. ———. *Proceso y contenido de la novela hispanoamericana.* 2d ed. Madrid: Gredos, 1968 (1953). 630 pp.

After a general discussion of the Spanish American novel, the author chronologically studies the novel from the colonial period to the twentieth century.

375. Sánchez Trencado, José Luis. *Literatura latinoamericana: Siglo XX.* Buenos Aires: A. Peña Lillo, 1964. 138 pp.

General view, with chapters treating specific authors.

376. Sanjuán, Pilar A. *El ensayo hispánico: Estudio y antología.* Madrid: Gredos, 1954. 412 pp.

Anthology as well as study of Spanish and Spanish American essayists. Good bibliography for each author as well as a general bibliography. Factual errors and poor introduction.

377. Saz Sánchez, Agustín del. *Teatro hispanoamericano.* Barcelona: Vergara, 1963–64. 2 vols.

Comprehensive general history of the Spanish American theater. Uneven treatment of authors, occasional poor organization of material, and absence of indexes.

378. Schulman, Ivan, Manuel Pedro González, Juan Loveluck, and Fernando Alegría. *Coloquio sobre la novela hispanoamericana.* Mexico: Fondo de Cultura Económica, 1967. 150 pp.

Studies the origin and nature of the new Spanish American novel and its relation to the world novel.

379. Schwartz, Kessel. *A New History of Spanish American Fiction.* Coral Gables, Fla.: University of Miami Press, 1972. 2 vols.

Volume 1 covers the literature from colonial times to the Mexican Revolution, and volume 2, which discusses social concern and universalism, is devoted largely to the study of the new novel. Contains copious notes, and extensive bibliography, and indexes of authors and titles. This is probably the most comprehensive historical-critical assessment of Spanish American fiction published to date.

380. Solórzano, Carlos. *Teatro latinoamericano del siglo XX.* Buenos Aires: Ediciones Nueva Visión, 1961. 105 pp. Mexico: Pormaca, 1964. 200 pp.

Guide to the twentieth-century theater. Includes information on the development of the university theater.

381. Spell, Jefferson Rea. *Contemporary Spanish American Fiction.* Chapel Hill: University of North Carolina Press, 1944. 323 pp.

One chapter is devoted to fiction prior to 1914. Gives detailed treatment of the works of a limited number of writers.

382. Stabb, Martin S. *In Quest of Identity: Patterns in the Spanish American Essay of Ideas.* Chapel Hill: University of North Carolina Press, 1967. 244 pp.

Ideological tendencies studied in essayists and political publicists. Covers the humanist reaction against science and the rediscovery of

America from 1920 on. Final chapters are devoted to Argentina and Mexico. Bibliography (pp. 221–33).

383. Stimson, Frederick S. *The New Schools of Spanish American Poetry.* Estudios de Hispanófila, vol. 13. Chapel Hill: University of North Carolina Press, 1970. 217 pp.

History of literary movements in modern poetry that attempts to define contemporary movements since modernism. Bibliography.

384. Suárez-Murias, Marguerite C. *La novela romántica en Hispanoamérica.* New York: Hispanic Institute, 1963. 247 pp.

About 10 to 15 pages devoted to the novel of each country. Emphasis on names, titles, dates, and plot summaries. Lengthy bibliography.

385. Torres-Ríoseco, Arturo. *The Epic of Latin American Literature.* 3d ed. Berkeley and Los Angeles: University of California Press, 1967 (1942). ix + 277 pp. Spanish version, *La gran literatura iberoamericana,* 2d ed. (Buenos Aires, 1951 [1945]). 320 pp.

Popular, concise history. One chapter is devoted to Brazilian literature. Major emphasis is on kinds of literature and broad themes, for example, novels of the city. Passages translated into English indicate the intention of reaching non-Spanish-speaking persons. Some errors of fact.

386. ———. *Grandes novelistas de la América hispana.* 2d ed. Berkeley and Los Angeles: University of California Press, 1949 (1941–43). 2 vols.

Basically the same work as *Novelistas contemporáneos de América* (see no. 388).

387. ———. *La novela en la América hispana.* 2d ed. Berkeley and Los Angeles: University of California Press, 1949 (1939). 255 pp.

A survey. Most attention given to those novels demonstrating local color.

388. ———. *Novelistas contemporáneos de América.* Santiago de Chile: Editorial Nascimiento, 1939. 422 pp.

Studies of the novels of 12 writers. Torres-Ríoseco characteristically divides the novels according to their setting, countryside or city, with a third category revealing the influence of *modernismo*.

389. ———. *Nueva historia de la gran literatura iberoamericana.* 6th ed. New York: Las Americas, 1966 (1945). 337 pp.

From the colonial period to the 1950s.

390. Torres-Ríoseco, Arturo, ed. *La novela iberoamericana: Memoria del Quinto Congreso del Instituto Internacional de Literatura*

Iberoamericana. Albuquerque: University of New Mexico Press, 1951. 212 pp.

A collection of 13 essays on the novel from colonial times to the present.

391. Ugarte, Manuel. *Escritores iberoamericanos de 1900.* 2d ed. Mexico: Editorial Vértice, 1947 (1942). 269 pp.

Chapters on 12 writers with general commentary on the literary scene.

392. Valbuena Briones, Angel. *Literatura hispanoamericana.* Vol. 5 of *Historia de la literatura española,* by Angel Valbuena Prat. 4th ed. Barcelona: Gustavo Gili, 1973 (1963). 668 pp.

An extensive overview of Spanish American literature from its beginnings to the contemporary period. A sound introduction to this literature.

393. Vitier, Medardo. *Del ensayo americano.* Mexico: Fondo de Cultura Económica, 1945. 292 pp.

Considers 12 essayists of Spanish America. Stresses the political and cultural background. Useful study.

394. Zum Felde, Alberto. *Los ensayistas.* Mexico: Guaranía, 1954. 606 pp.

The first of a two-volume study under the title of *Indice crítico de la literatura hispanoamericana.* Very extensive study of the essay from colonial times to the present. Includes a wide variety of writers such as Cortés, Bello, Korn, and Anderson-Imbert.

395. ———. *Indice crítico de la literatura hispanoamericana.* 2 vols. Vol. 2, *La narrativa.* Mexico: Guaranía, 1959.

History of the novel in Spanish America. Excellent index indicates content of each chapter. The first volume treats the essay.

National (alphabetized by country)

Consult chapter 9 (pp. 88–102) for anthologies of Spanish America, since these books frequently have introductory studies, biobibliographic information, and notes.

Argentina

396. Arrieta, Rafael Alberto. *La literatura argentina y sus vínculos con España.* Buenos Aires: Impresora Francisco A. Colombo, 1957. 205 pp.

A concise history from the late 1770s to this century, interpreting the works as they relate to Argentine history, world events, and other literatures.

397. Arrieta, Rafael Alberto, ed. *Historia de la literatura argentina.* Buenos Aires: Peuser, 1958–60. 6 vols.

Done in collaboration with many writers, some of them well-known critics. Comprehensive coverage of all genres and all periods from 1516 on, relating them to world literature and events. Detailed footnotes.

398. Berenguer Carisomo, Arturo. *Las ideas estéticas en el teatro argentino.* Buenos Aires: Comisión Nacional de Cultura, Instituto Nacional de Estudios de Teatro, 1947. 438 pp.

Somewhat nebulous discussion of the Argentine theater from pre-Columbian times to 1919.

399. Blanco Amores de Pagella, Angela. *Nuevos temas en el teatro argentino: La influencia europea.* Huemul, 1965. 185 pp.

Careful analysis of such influences as the *sainete,* Pirandello, expressionism, Brecht, Beckett, Greek myth.

400. Castagnino, Raúl H. *Literatura dramática argentina (1717–1967).* Buenos Aires: Pleamar, 1968. 208 pp.

Outline history, which is, however, the best source for up-to-date information on the Argentine theater. This is a somewhat revised and substantially updated version of Castagnino's *Esquema de la literatura dramática argentina* (1950).

401. Castellanos, Luis Arturo. *El cuento en la Argentina.* Santa Fe: Editorial Colmegna, 1967. 64 pp.

A brief, superficial study of the modern short story in Argentina. The work is designed to orient the reader to a few of the general trends.

402. Foppa, Tito L. *Diccionario teatral del Río de la Plata.* Buenos Aires: Ediciones Carro de Tespis, 1961. 1,046 pp.

Biographies of Argentine dramatists; history of Argentine theater; and lists of associations of authors, dramatists, composers, and artists.

403. García, Germán. *La novela argentina: Un itinerario.* Buenos Aires: Sudamericana, 1952. 317 pp.

Guide to the development of Argentine prose fiction. Treats the *cuento* and the *relato breve* as well as the novel.

404. Ghiano, Juan Carlos. *Poesía argentina del siglo XX.* Mexico: Fondo de Cultura Económica, 1957. 285 pp.

Ninety-two poets are treated succinctly. The last 80 to 90 pages are more a directory than a selective study. The material is arranged according to three main categories: modernism, imagism, and neoromanticism.

405. ————. *Testimonio de la novela argentina*. Buenos Aires: Leviatán, 1956. 187 pp.

Payró, Güiraldes, and Arlt are among the authors treated in this study.

406. Lichtblau, Myron I. *The Argentine Novel in the Nineteenth Century*. New York: Hispanic Institute, 1959. 225 pp.

Thorough coverage of material. Chronological list of novels. Much bibliographical information.

407. Magis, Carlos Horacio. *La literatura argentina*. Mexico: Editorial Pormaca, 1965. 307 pp.

In nine chapters the author traces briefly the development of Argentine literature from 1516 to 1960, fixing attention on the most representative writers of each period. He considers effects on literature of political, educational, social, and economic changes.

408. Mastrángelo, Carlos. *El cuento argentino: Contribución al conocimiento de su historia, teoría y práctica*. Buenos Aires: Hachette, 1963. 132 pp.

An analysis of Argentine short-story anthologies from Manuel Gálvez's *Los mejores cuentos* (1919) to Mignon Domínguez's *16 cuentos argentinos* (1957); brief comments on unanthologized authors (at the time) like Martínez Estrada and Borges; and some theoretical considerations.

409. Ordaz, Luis. *El teatro en el Río de la Plata desde sus orígenes hasta nuestros días*. 2d ed. Buenos Aires: Leviatán, 1957 (1946). 233 pp.

From primitive Indian dances and festivities to modern period.

410. Percas, Helena. *La poesía femenina argentina (1810–1950)*. Madrid: Cultura Hispánica, 1958. 738 pp.

Major emphasis on the poetesses since the generation of 1916, that is, since Alfonsina Storni. Extensive bibliography.

411. Pinto, Juan. *Panorama de la literatura argentina contemporánea*. Buenos Aires: Angel Estrada, 1955. 382 pp.

Brief treatment of each author with bibliography, commentary, and evaluations by other critics.

412. Rojas, Ricardo. *Historia de la literatura argentina*. 4th ed. Buenos Aires: Kraft, 1957 (1917). 9 vols.

From the colonial era to the end of nineteenth century. Extensive coverage. A factual, historical approach to Argentine literature by an eminent critic.

413. Williams Alzaga, Enrique. *La pampa en la novela argentina.* Buenos Aires: Angel Estrada, 1955. 382 pp.

Description of the pampa, travelers' impressions of the pampa, and its role in the novel and also the short story.

Bolivia

414. Díez de Medina, Fernando. *Literatura boliviana: Introducción al estudio de las letras nacionales del tiempo mítico a la producción contemporánea.* Madrid: Aguilar, 1959. 416 pp.

Gives social picture of each period. Concentrates on principal authors. From indigenous myths to contemporary period.

415. Finot, Enrique. *Historia de la literatura boliviana (desde sus orígenes hasta 1942).* 3d ed. La Paz: Gisbert, 1964 (1945). 622 pp.

Extensive study of Bolivian literature. No bibliography.

416. Guzmán, Augusto. *La novela en Bolivia: Proceso, 1847–1954.* La Paz: Juventud, 1955. 180 pp.

Revision and enlargement of author's book by the same title published in 1938. Covers the romantics (1847–1905), the realists (1905–32), and the naturalists (1932–54).

Chile

417. Alegría, Fernando. *La literatura chilena del siglo XX.* 2d ed. Santiago: Zig-Zag, 1967. 287 pp.

First part offers an overall view, while the second is divided into discussions of writings in prose and poetry.

418. ———. *La poesía chilena: Orígenes y desarrollo del siglo XVI al XIX.* Mexico: Fondo de Cultura Económica; Berkeley and Los Angeles: University of California Press, 1954. xiii + 312 pp.

Comprehensive study with bibliography.

419. Campbell, Margaret V. *The Development of the National Theater in Chile to 1842.* Gainesville: University of Florida Press, 1958. v + 78 pp.

Also includes a select bibliography on Chilean theater.

420. Cánepa Guzmán, Mario. *El teatro en Chile: Desde los indios hasta los teatros universitarios.* Santiago: Arancibia Hermanos Editores, 1966. 135 pp.

The orientation is historical rather than aesthetic. The bibliography is brief, and there are no indexes. The "Epoca Actual" is devoted almost entirely to Acevedo Hernández, Moock, and lists of drama prizes.

421. Castillo, Homero. *El criollismo en la novela chilena.* Mexico: Ediciones de Andrea, 1962. 110 pp.

Study of an important aspect of the Chilean novel. Good bibliography.

422. Díaz Arrieta, Hernán ("Alone"). *Los cuatro grandes de la literatura chilena del siglo XX.* Santiago: Zig-Zag, 1963. 234 pp.

Studies Augusto D'Halmar, Pedro Prado, Gabriela Mistral, and Pablo Neruda.

423. ———. *Historia personal de la literatura chilena, desde don Alonso de Ercilla hasta Pablo Neruda.* 2d ed. Santiago: Zig-Zag, 1962 (1954). 669 pp.

Contains a biographical dictionary of authors and an anthology of twentieth-century authors.

424. Goić, Cedomil. *La novela chilena: Los mitos degradados.* Santiago: Imprenta Universitaria, 1968. 214 pp.

Among the eight nineteenth- and twentieth-century novels analyzed are Blest Gana's *Martín Rivas,* M. Romas's *Hijo de ladrón,* M. L. Bombal's *Ultima niebla,* and J. Donoso's *Coronación.*

425. Medina, José Toribio. *Historia de la literatura colonial de Chile.* Santiago: Librería del Mercurio, 1878. 3 vols.

Classic study by an eminent scholar.

426. Rojas, Manuel. *Historia breve de la literatura chilena.* Santiago: Zig-Zag, 1965. 202 pp.

A good general overview of Chilean literature.

427. ———. *Manual de literatura chilena.* Mexico: Universidad Nacional Autónoma de México, 1964. 152 pp.

A concise, elementary manual comprising five chapters that recount chronologically the evolution of Chilean letters.

428. Silva Castro, Raúl. *Historia crítica de la novela chilena, 1843–1956.* Madrid: Cultura Hispánica, 1960. 425 pp. Previous version, *Panorama de la novela chilena (1843–1953)* (Mexico: Fondo de Cultura Económica, 1955). 224 pp.

From precursors to contemporaries, with comprehensive introduction and critical bibliography at end of each chapter.

429. ———. *Panorama literario de Chile.* Santiago: Editorial Universitaria, 1961. 570 pp.

Comprehensive coverage. Much attention is given to younger

writers. Useful appendixes on such topics as the literary world of 1842 and Rubén Darío's presence in Chile.

430. Torres-Ríoseco, Arturo. *Breve historia de la literatura chilena.* Mexico: Ediciones de Andrea, 1956. 175 pp.

Concise study that covers sixteenth through twentieth centuries.

431. Urbistondo, Vicente. *El naturalismo en la novela chilena.* Santiago: Andrés Bello, 1966. 197 pp.

Useful contribution to the study of the Chilean novel.

Colombia

432. Botero, Ebel. *Cinco poetas colombianos: Estudios sobre Silva, Valencia, Luis Carlos López, Rivera, y Maya.* Manizales: Imprenta Departamental, 1964. 270 pp.

433. Caparroso, Carlos Arturo. *Dos ciclos de lirismo colombiano.* Bogota: Instituto Caro y Cuervo, 1961. 213 pp.

A history of Colombian poetry of the nineteenth and early twentieth centuries which is marred by a lack of historical sense. It contains biographical sketches and bibliographies.

434. Curcio Altamar, Antonio. *Evolución de la novela en Colombia.* Bogota: Instituto Caro y Cuervo, 1957. xxviii + 339 pp.

Studies the novel from the colonial period to the twentieth century. Relates Colombian novels to those of other American countries and Europe. Extensive bibliography.

435. Gómez Restrepo, Antonio. *Historia de la literatura colombiana.* 3d ed. Bogota: Imprenta Nacional de Colombia, 1953–54 (1938–46). 4 vols.

This history covers only the colonial period and poetry of the nineteenth century. Author includes many passages from original works; for example, 75 pages are devoted to the writings of Madre Francisca Josefa del Castillo.

436. McGrady, Donald. *La novela histórica en Colombia.* Bogota: Kelly, 1962. 189 pp.

Studies 29 historical novels, 25 of which have American themes.

437. Núñez Segura, José A. *Literatura colombiana: Sinopsis y comentarios de autores representativos.* 5th ed. Medellín: Bedout, 1961. 627 pp.

Synopsis of historical events; authors' biographies; accounts of literary movements; studies of novels, short stories, oratory, theater, journalism, and so forth. Also includes catalog of writers and their works, and excerpts from many works and analyses of same.

438. Ortega Torres, José J. *Historia de la literatura colombiana.* 2d ed. Bogota: Cromos, 1935 (1934). xl + 1,214 pp.

From 1538 to 1934. Many minor authors included. Passages from works of all authors.

439. Otero Muñoz, Gustavo. *Historia de la literatura colombiana.* 5th ed. Bogota: Editorial Voluntad, 1943 (1935). 334 pp.

General treatment of Colombian literature.

440. Sanín Cano, Baldomero. *Letras colombianas.* Mexico: Fondo de Cultura Económica, 1944. 213 pp.

Concise reference to chief authors from the colonial period to 1941.

441. Vergara y Vergara, José María. *Historia de la literatura en Nueva Granada: Desde la conquista hasta la independencia (1538–1820).* 4th ed. Bogota: ABC, 1958 (1867). 3 vols.

Well-known work. Notes by A. Gómez Restrepo and G. Otero Muñoz. Lengthy indexes of various subject matter are very helpful.

Costa Rica

442. Bonilla, Abelardo. *Historia de la literatura costarricense.* San José: Editorial Costa Rica, 1967. 408 pp.

Panoramic history of Costa Rican literature, which acquired depth in the twentieth century. The essay is considered the most cultivated genre today.

Cuba

443. Arrom, José Juan. *Historia de la literatura dramática cubana.* New Haven, Conn.: Yale University Press, 1944. 1,332 pp.

Extensive coverage of Cuban theater from 1512 to 1942. Good bibliography.

444. Bueno, Salvador. *Historia de la literatura cubana (1902–1952).* 3d ed. Havana: Ministerio de Educación, 1963 (1953). 459 pp.

Evolution of Cuban literature with reading selections.

445. González Freire, Natividad. *Teatro cubano, 1928–1961.* Havana: Ministerio de Relaciones Exteriores, 1961. 181 pp.

The author carefully studies each group, applying Petersen's theory of generations and analyzing the work of each author in some detail. References and notes are included.

446. Henríquez Ureña, Max. *Panorama histórico de la literatura cubana.* New York: Las Americas, 1963. 2 vols.

Cuban literature viewed against the background of its history.

447. Jiménez, José O. *Estudios sobre poesía cubana contemporánea.*
New York: Las Americas, 1967. 113 pp.
Studies Boti, Acosta, Florit, Gaztelu, and Fernández Retamar.

448. Lazo, Raimundo. *La literatura cubana.* Mexico: Universidad
Nacional Autónoma de México, 1965. 254 pp.
Schematic history from its beginnings to 1964.

449. Olivera, Otto. *Cuba en su poesía.* Mexico: Ediciones de Andrea,
1965. 217 pp.
Author limits himself to regionalistic and nationalistic themes.
Studies Cuban poetry from the *Espejo de paciencia* (1608) through
the nineteenth century. A final chapter summarizes the first 60 years
of the twentieth century.

450. Remos y Rubio, Juan J. *Historia de la literatura cubana.*
Havana: Cárdenas, 1945. 3 vols.
From the sixteenth to the twentieth century.

Dominican Republic

451. Balaguer, Joaquín. *Literatura dominicana.* Buenos Aires: Editorial Americalee, 1950. 365 pp.
Studies of 25 authors, all of whom were born in the nineteenth
century.

452. Henríquez Ureña, Max. *Panorama histórico de la literatura
dominicana.* Rio de Janeiro: Compañía Brasileira de Artes Gráficos,
1945. 337 pp.
Good introduction. From first literary manifestations to contemporary period. Revised edition published in Santo Domingo (1965).

Ecuador

453. Barrera, Isaac J. *Historia de la literatura ecuatoriana.* 2d ed.
Quito: Editorial Ecuatoriana, 1953–55 (1944). 4 vols.
Ecuadorian literature from pre-Columbian and colonial epochs to
the middle of the twentieth century. Abundant bibliographic sources.

454. Carrera Andrade, Jorge. *Galería de místicos y de insurgentes.*
Quito: Casa de la Cultura Ecuatoriana, 1959. 190 pp.
Ecuadorian intellectual and literary activity between 1555 and
1955.

455. Descalzi, Ricardo. *Historia crítica del teatro ecuatoriano.* Quito:
Casa de la Cultura Ecuatoriana, 1968. 6 vols.
Half of volume 1 (125 pp.) is a history of the Ecuadorian theater,
and the remaining 5½ volumes treat individual authors chronolog-

ically by year of first play. Over 75 percent of the total is devoted to the twentieth century. Evaluations of about 125 authors and close to 600 plays.

456. Rojas, Angel F. *La novela ecuatoriana.* Mexico: Fondo de Cultura Económica, 1948. 234 pp.

Provides a sociopolitical background for the history of the Ecuadorian novel. Brief consideration of authors and works. Bibliography.

El Salvador

457. Gallegos Valdés, Luis. *Panorama de la literatura salvadoreña.* 2d ed. San Salvador: Ministerio de Educación, 1962 (1958). 238 pp.

Lacks organization and perspective in attempting to cover the whole literary history of El Salvador.

458. Toruño, Juan Felipe. *Desarrollo literario de El Salvador: Ensayo cronológico de generaciones y etapas de las letras salvadoreñas.* San Salvador: Ministerio de Cultura, Departamento Editorial, 1957. 440 pp.

Prolix panoramic view of Salvadorean literature which often degenerates into mere listings of authors and works.

Guatemala

459. Menton, Seymour. *Historia crítica de la novela guatemalteca.* Guatemala: Editorial Universitaria, 1960. 335 pp.

General view of Guatemalan novel. Analyses of the works of the most important writers, for example, Milla, Asturias, and Monteforte Toledo.

460. Vela, David. *Literatura guatemalteca.* 3d ed. Guatemala: Tipografía Nacional, 1948 (1943). 2 vols.

Lengthy treatment of Guatemalan literature from indigenous period to the twentieth century.

Mexico

461. Azuela, Mariano. *Cien años de novela mexicana.* Mexico: Botas, 1947. 226 pp.

Study of the most important Mexican novelists between the War of Independence and the Revolution.

462. Brushwood, John S. *Mexico in Its Novel: A Nation's Search for Identity.* Austin and London: University of Texas Press, 1966. 292 pp.

Mexican reality revealed through the nation's novel. Covers period 1521–1963. Also contains a chronological list of Mexican novels (1832–1963) on which organization of book is based, a selected bibliography, and an index.

463. ———. *The Romantic Novel in Mexico.* Columbia: University of Missouri Press, 1954. 98 pp.

A sound introductory study with bibliography.

464. Brushwood, John S., and José Rojas Garciadueñas. *Breve historia de la novela mexicana.* Mexico: Ediciones de Andrea, 1959. 157 pp.

This useful student manual provides a brief introduction to authors together with a bibliography. From origins to 1959.

465. Dauster, Frank. *Breve historia de la poesía mexicana.* Mexico: Ediciones de Andrea, 1963. 198 pp.

Covers all movements of Mexican poetry from pre-Hispanic times. Brief annotated bibliography.

466. González, Manuel Pedro. *Trayectoria de la novela en México.* Mexico: Botas, 1951. 418 pp.

The evolution of the novel as revealed in its most prominent stages, schools, and individual works. The result is a rather comprehensive history.

467. González Peña, Carlos. *Historia de la literatura mexicana: Desde los orígenes hasta nuestros días.* 9th ed. Mexico: Porrúa, 1966 (1928). 349 pp. English translation, *History of Mexican Literature,* by Gusta Barfield Nance and Florence Johnson Dunstan, 3d ed. (Dallas, Tex.: Southern Methodist University Press, 1968 [1943]). 398 pp.

A standard study that provides general critical evaluation of important literary works and movements.

468. Haneffstengel, Renate von. *El México de hoy en la novela y el cuento.* Mexico: Ediciones de Andrea, 1966. 113 pp.

Includes Yáñez, Fuentes, Castellanos, Rulfo, Rojas González, and Spota.

469. Jiménez Rueda, Julio. *Historia de la literatura mexicana.* 5th ed. Mexico: Botas, 1960 (1928). 387 pp.

From the indigenous period to the present. Chronological table of literary events. Good bibliography.

470. ———. *Letras mexicanas en el siglo XIX.* Mexico: Fondo de Cultura Económica, 1944. 189 pp.

Emphasis on movements, history, and society. A clear presentation of trends, but there are no sharp critical analyses of literary works.

471. Langford, Walter M. *The Mexican Novel Comes of Age*. Notre Dame, Ind.: University of Notre Dame Press, 1971. 229 pp.

Brief summary of the Mexican novel prior to the twentieth century. Covers Azuela and his disciples, Traven, Yáñez, Rulfo, Spota, Fuentes, and others. Selective general and special bibliographies for each chapter.

472. Leal, Luis. *Breve historia del cuento mexicano*. Mexico: Ediciones de Andrea, 1956. 163 pp.

Covers all epochs from the pre-Hispanic to the middle of this century. Brief treatment of authors with essential bibliographic information.

473. Magaña Esquivel, Antonio, and Ruth S. Lamb. *Breve historia del teatro mexicano*. Mexico: Ediciones de Andrea, 1958. 176 pp.

Concise study with a good deal of bibliography.

474. María y Campos, Armando de. *El teatro de género chico en la revolución mexicana*. Mexico: Biblioteca del Instituto Nacional de Estudios Históricos de la Revolución Mexicana, 1956. 439 pp.

Studies the *género chico* from 1901 to 1956.

475. Martínez, José Luis. *Literatura mexicana, siglo XX*. Mexico: Robredo, 1949–50. 2 vols.

Part 1 consists of a lengthy series of studies on a wide variety of topics. The second part constitutes a major contribution to a bibliography of Mexican letters and, in particular, to literary journals.

476. Morton, F. Rand. *Los novelistas de la revolución mexicana*. Mexico: Editorial Cultura, 1949. 270 pp.

Very detailed, informative presentation of 13 novelists of the Mexican Revolution. Other authors are mentioned briefly.

477. Navarro, Joaquina. *La novela realista mexicana*. Mexico: Compañía General de Ediciones, 1955. 333 pp.

Detailed study of Mexican society as seen in the works of major and minor novelists of the realistic period. Bibliography.

478. Olavarría y Ferrari, Enrique de. *Reseña histórica del teatro en México*. Prologue by Salvador Novo. Mexico: Porrúa, 1961. 5 vols.

It includes the author's unpublished manuscript for the years 1896–1911 as well as a month-by-month listing for 1911–61 prepared by David Arce. Material from two previous editions (1880 and 1895) is also included. A recent index to this work is *Indices a la reseña histórica del teatro en México* (1538–1911) *de Enrique de*

Olavarría y Ferrari, Bibliografía mexicana, no. 4 (Mexico: Porrúa, 1968).

479. Read, John L. *The Mexican Historical Novel, 1826–1910.* New York: Instituto de las Españas, 1939. xiv + 337 pp.

Provides information on literary trends and their influence on the historical novel. Bibliography of novels and critical studies.

480. Rojas Garcidueñas, José J. *El teatro de Nueva España en el siglo XVI.* Mexico: Luis Alvarez, 1935. 228 pp.

Outline history of early Mexican theater. Appendix contains some theatrical pieces.

481. Sommers, Joseph. *After the Storm: Landmarks of the Modern Novel.* Albuquerque: University of New Mexico Press, 1968. xii + 208 pp. Spanish version, *Yáñez, Rulfo, Fuentes: La novela mexicana* (Caracas: Monte Avila, 1970). 240 pp.

Mainly studies Yáñez, Rulfo, and Fuentes. Includes bibliographic references.

482. Urbina, Luis Gonzaga. *La vida literaria de México y la literatura mexicana durante la guerra de la independencia.* Mexico: Porrúa, 1946. xii + 407 pp.

Two major studies by Urbina which serve as a history of literature. The period of the War of Independence is well covered.

483. Valenzuela Rodarte, Alberto. *Historia de la literatura en México.* Mexico: Editorial Jus, 1961. 623 pp.

Development of Mexican literature from the indigenous period to the 1950s.

484. Warner, Ralph E. *Historia de la novela mexicana en el siglo XIX.* Mexico: Robredo, 1953. 130 pp.

Work of synthesis which gives essential facts, critical evaluations, and bibliography.

Nicaragua

485. Ycaza Tigerino, Julio César. *La poesía y los poetas de Nicaragua.* Managua: Academia Nicaragüense de la Lengua, 1958. 148 pp.

Panama

486. García S., Ismael. *Historia de la literatura panameña.* Mexico: Universidad Nacional Autónoma de México, 1964. 189 pp.

Manual for university students. Bibliography.

487. Miró, Rodrigo. *La literatura panameña (origen y proceso).* Panama, 1970. 231 pp.

The first part treats the literature of conquest (1502–1821), the second extends from the colonial period to the republic (1821–1903), and the third and longest part covers Panamanian literature during the years 1903–70. Bibliography.

Paraguay

488. Centurión, Carlos R. *Historia de las letras paraguayas.* Buenos Aires: Ayacucho, 1947–51. 3 vols.

First serious attempt at a systematic study of Paraguayan letters from the colonial period to the middle of the twentieth century. Much politico-cultural history in addition to literature.

489. Pérez-Maricevich, Francisco. *La poesía y la narrativa en el Paraguay.* Asunción: Editorial del Centenario, 1969. 72 pp.

While this critical analysis of Paraguayan literature rejects the notion of a literary tradition in Paraguay, the author rightfully focuses on the better achievements of Gabriel Casaccia and Augusto Roa Bastos. First part of this study is a reprint of *Poesía y conciencia de la poesía en el Paraguay* (Asunción: Ediciones Epoca, 1967).

490. Plá, Josefina. *El teatro en el Paraguay: Primera parte, de la fundación a 1870.* Asunción: Editorial Diálogo, 1967. 90 pp.

Volume 1 of the second edition of the author's *Cuatro siglos de teatro en el Paraguay* (Asunción, 1966). A careful and documented study. Contains bibliography.

491. Rodríguez Alcalá, Hugo. *Historia de la literatura paraguaya.* Mexico: Ediciones de Andrea, 1970. 199 pp.

Concise history from the colonial period to the twentieth century. Ample bibliography.

492. Velázquez, Rafael Eladio. *Breve historia de la cultura en el Paraguay.* Curitiba (Brazil): Editorial Lítero-tenica, 1966. 328 pp.

Textbook that deals chronologically with the education, culture, arts and letters, and sciences of Paraguay.

Peru

493. Aldrich, Earl M., Jr. *The Modern Short Story in Peru.* Madison: University of Wisconsin Press, 1966. xi + 212 pp.

Study of the twentieth-century Peruvian short story. Stresses importance of the *modernista* movement in the development of this genre. Aldrich considers Alegría and J. M. Arguedas to be pivotal figures. Good bibliography.

494. Castro Arenas, Mario. *La novela peruana y la evolución social.* Lima: Ediciones Cultura y Libertad, 1965. 286 pp.

The development of the Peruvian novel as related to its society. Begins with *El Lazarillo de ciegos caminantes* and extends to the present. Much attention given to nineteenth-century novelists, but too sketchy for the twentieth century.

495. Monguió, Luis. *La poesía postmodernista peruana.* Berkeley and Los Angeles: University of California Press; Mexico: Fondo de Cultura Económica, 1954. 253 pp.

Careful scholarship. Bibliography on Peruvian poetry from 1915 to 1950 covers 33 pages.

496. Nieto, Luis Carlos. *Poetas y escritores peruanos.* Cuzco: Editorial Sol y Piedra, 1957. 72 pp.

Biocritical notes on nine of Peru's outstanding writers, among whom are: Santos Chocano, Clorinda Matto de Turner, José Díaz Canseco, Ricardo Palma, and César Vallejo.

497. Sánchez, Luis Alberto. *La literatura del Perú.* 2d ed. Buenos Aires: Imprenta de Buenos Aires, 1943 (1939). 189 pp.

Volume 1 of a two-volume collection called *Las literaturas américas.* Emphasis on sociological, historical background. Bibliography of basic titles of Peruvian literature.

498. ———. *La literatura peruana: Derrotero para una historia espiritual del Perú.* 2d ed. Buenos Aires and Asunción: Guaranía, 1966 (1950). 6 vols.

From the time of the Incas to the present as seen through the influence of the geography and culture of the Indians and Spaniards. Literature is viewed as a spiritual voice of the people. Much bibliographic information.

499. Tamayo Vargas, Augusto. *Literatura peruana.* Lima: Universidad Nacional Mayor de San Marcos, 1965. 2 vols.

From pre-Columbian literature to the present. Useful bibliography.

Puerto Rico

500. Manrique Cabrera, Francisco. *Historia de la literatura puertorriqueña.* New York: Las Americas, 1956. 384 pp.

Panoramic view of Puerto Rican literature from the sixteenth century to the present.

501. Pasarrel, Emilio J. *Orígenes y desarrollo de la afición treatral en Puerto Rico.* Reprint of pts. 1 (1951) and 2 (1967). San Juan: Editorial Universitaria, 1970. 463 pp.

The standard source on the subject. Important for its facts and not its critical comments. Part 2 is a summary of activity on the stage from 1900 to 1962.

502. Phillips, Jordan B. *Contemporary Puerto Rican Drama.* Madrid: Plaza Mayor Ediciones, 1972. 216 pp.

Covers the years 1938–68. Bibliography of books and articles. Also includes an index of plays discussed.

503. Rivera de Alvarez, Josefina. *Historia de la literatura puertorriqueña.* Santurce: Departamento de Instrucción Pública, 1969. 2 vols.

Intended as a text for high school and university students. Comprises eight chapters, each with a historical-cultural introduction. Contains an end vocabulary, notes, and bibliography.

504. Rosa-Nieves, Cesáreo. *Aguinaldo lírico de la poesía puertorriqueña.* Rev. ed. Río Piedras: Edil, 1971 (1957). 3 vols.

Volume 1 covers romantics and Parnassians (1843–1907), volume 2 the modernists (1907–21), and volume 3 the postmodernists and vanguardists (1921–56). Brief bibliographic introduction to each author.

Uruguay

505. Benedetti, Mario. *Literatura uruguaya: Siglo XX.* Montevideo: Alfa, 1963. 174 pp.

A collection of essays on contemporary Uruguayan letters. Most are concerned with specific authors and aspects of their work. One essay comments on recent literary trends in Uruguay.

506. Bollo, Sarah. *Literatura uruguaya, 1807–1965.* Montevideo: Orfeo, 1965. 2 vols.

Biobibliography of the literature of Uruguay.

Englekirk and Ramos. *La narrativa uruguaya.* See no. 166.

507. Rela, Walter. *Historia del teatro uruguayo, 1808–1968.* Montevideo: Banda Oriental, 1969. 187 pp.

A good overview of the Uruguayan theater. Bibliography.

508. Reyles, Carlos, ed. *Historia sintética de la literatura uruguaya.* Montevideo: Alfredo Vila, 1931. 3 vols.

A series of 26 essays by 25 critics covering Uruguayan literature of all periods.

509. Roxlo, Carlos. *Historia crítica de la literatura uruguaya.* Montevideo: A. Barreiro y Ramos, 1912–16. 7 vols. Later ed., 1936.

Very extensive coverage from the period of Independence to 1916.

510. Zum Felde, Alberto. *La literatura del Uruguay.* 2d ed. Vol. 2 of *Las literaturas américas* (2 vols.). Montevideo: Colorado, 1941 (1939).

From colonial period to about 1935. Brief bibliography.

511. ———. *Proceso intelectual del Uruguay y crítica de la literatura uruguaya.* Montevideo: Editorial del Nuevo Mundo, 1967. 3 vols.

From the end of the colonial period to the contemporary period. Treats a vast number of authors but gives considerable attention to the few major ones.

Venezuela

512. Angarita Arvelo, Rafael. *Historia y crítica de la novela en Venezuela.* Berlin: August Fries Leipzig, 1938. 173 pp.

Brief survey of the development of the novel in Venezuela.

513. Araujo, Orlando. *Narrativa venezolana contemporánea.* Caracas: Editorial Tiempo Nuevo, 1972. 355 pp.

Treats best such writers as Gallegos, Meneses, Uslar Pietri, Otero Silva, and González León but insufficiently covers most of the newest writers. Some of the later chapters have some thematic unity: the novel of violence (chapter 7) and the narratives dealing with the problems of present-day Venezuelan youth (chapter 12).

514. Díaz Siejas, Pedro. *La antigua y la moderna literatura venezolana: Estudio histórico-crítico con antología.* Caracas: Ediciones Armitano, 1966. 782 pp.

Evolution of Venezuelan letters with representative selections from many authors. Valuable bibliography for each chapter.

515. Medina, José Ramón. *50 años de literatura venezolana.* Caracas: Monte Avila, 1972. 324 pp.

Very general history from 1918 to 1968.

516. Picón-Febres, Gonzalo. *La literatura venezolana en el siglo diez y nueve.* 2d ed. Buenos Aires: Ayacucho, 1947 (1906). 443 pp.

Stresses historical setting, society, and reviews of the period.

517. Picón Salas, Mariano. *Estudios de literatura venezolana.* Caracas and Madrid: Edime, 1961. 320 pp.

From the Spanish conquest to the present. Focuses on the spirit of the Venezuelans as revealed through their literature. Emphasis on twentieth-century authors.

518. ———. *Formación y proceso de la literatura venezolana.* Caracas: Cecilio Acosta, 1940. 271 pp.

Outline history from conquest to 1940. Extensive bibliography of literature from 1930 to 1940. Brief general bibliography.

519. Ratcliff, Dillwyn F. *Venezuelan Prose Fiction.* New York: Instituto de las Españas, 1933. 286 pp. Spanish version, *La prosa de ficción en Venezuela* (Caracas: Universidad Central, 1966). 278 pp.

History of the novel, sketch, and short story from the middle of the nineteenth century to the 1920s. Plots of some unattainable works summarized.

520. Rivera Silvestrini, José. *El cuento moderno venezolano.* Río Piedras: Editorial Cultura, 1967. 186 pp.

The development of the Venezuelan short story from the period of modernism (1890s) to around 1960. General bibliography and extensive bibliography on the writers included.

Literary Movements

See also chapter 7, pp. 51–52, for books on modernism.

Anderson. *Spanish American Modernism.* See no. 80.

521. Arguello, Santiago. *Modernismo y modernistas.* Guatemala: Tipografía Nacional, 1935. 2 vols.

Studies devoted mainly to Silva, Gutiérrez Nájera, Blanco Fombona, Darío, Nervo, and Arévalo Martínez.

522. Blanco-Fombona, Rufino. *El modernismo y los poetas modernistas.* Madrid: Editorial Mundo Latino, 1929. 364 pp.

Study of major poets of the various stages of the modernist movement. Quotes rather extensively from modernist poetry.

523. Bollo, Sarah. *El modernismo en el Uruguay.* Montevideo: Impresora Uruguaya, 1951. 141 pp.

Defines modernism and surveys criticism dealing with the movement.

524. Carilla, Emilio. *La literatura barroca en Hispanoamérica.* New York: Anaya, 1972. 209 pp.

The literary and historical development of the baroque in Latin America. Brief treatment of the neobaroque in contemporary Spanish American narrative.

525. ———. *El romanticismo en la América hispánica.* 2d ed. Madrid: Gredos, 1967 (1958). 2 vols.

Covers all aspects of romanticism (political, social, economic, European influences, themes, and language) in Spanish America and Brazil.

526. Castillo, Homero, ed. *Estudios críticos sobre el modernismo.* Madrid: Gredos, 1968. 416 pp.

A collection of essays by outstanding critics on modernism in Spain and Spanish America. Introduction, selection, and general bibliography by Homero Castillo.

527. Corvalán, Octavio. *Modernismo y vanguardia: Coordinadas de la literatura hispanoamericana del siglo XX.* New York: Las Americas, 1967. 263 pp.

   Treats the poetry and novel of the "heirs" of modernism and the poetry, essay, and novel of the vanguardists.

528. ———. *El postmodernismo.* New York: Las Americas, 1961. 159 pp.

   Focuses on major writers of the period between the world wars. Some important writers are omitted.

529. Craig, George Dundas. *The Modernist Trend in Spanish-American Poetry.* Berkeley and Los Angeles: University of California Press, 1934. 347 pp. Reprint, New York: Gordian Press, 1971.

   Introductory chapter on the modernist trend in Spanish American poetry, an anthology of representative poetry with English translations in verse, and commentaries. Short bibliography.

530. Davison, Ned J. *The Concept of Modernism in Hispanic Criticism.* Boulder, Colo.: Pruett Press, 1966. 188 pp. Spanish version, *El concepto de modernismo en la crítica hispánica* (Buenos Aires: Nova, 1971). 107 pp.

   Description of the concept of modernism with emphasis on poetry. Useful bibliography.

531. Fein, John M. *Modernismo in Chilean Literature: The Second Period.* Durham, N.C.: Duke University Press, 1965. x + 167 pp.

   The "second period" occurred after the departure of Darío from Chile. Two journals are given extensive treatment: *Revista cómica* and *Pluma y lápiz.* A chapter is devoted to the role of Francisco Contreras.

532. Fogelquist, Donald F. *Españoles de América y americanos de España.* Madrid: Gredos, 1968. 348 pp.

   Modernism as a Hispanic phenomenon in poetry and prose. Attention is mostly given to Spanish American modernists.

533. Henríquez Ureña, Max. *Breve historia del modernismo.* 2d ed. Mexico: Fondo de Cultura Económica, 1962 (1954). 559 pp.

   General view of modernism with chapters on more important writers. Good bibliography.

534. Loprete, Carlos. *La literatura modernista en la Argentina.* Buenos Aires: Poseidón, 1955. 126 pp.

80   *Histories of Spanish American Literature*

Brief survey. Includes journals, polemics, precursors, and major figures of modernism in Argentina, especially Larreta and Lugones.

535. Schulman, Ivan A. *Génesis del modernismo.* 2d ed. St. Louis, Mo.: Washington University Press, 1971 (1966). 224 pp.

Studies on early manifestations of modernist literature with special emphasis on Martí, Silva, and Casal.

536. Schulman, Ivan A., and Manuel Pedro González. *Martí, Darío y el modernismo.* Madrid: Gredos, 1969. 268 pp.

Schulman contributes a chapter defining modernism, and the remaining chapters deal with works of Martí and Darío.

537. Torres-Ríoseco, Arturo. *Precursores del modernismo.* Madrid: Espasa-Calpe, 1925. 125 pp.

Introduction to modernism and essays on four major writers: Casal, Gutiérrez Nájera, Martí, and Silva.

9   Anthologies

Spain and Spanish America

538. Abreu Gómez, Ermilo, ed. *Bellas, claras y sencillas páginas de la literatura castellana* (*España e Hispanoamérica*). Mexico: B. Costa-Amec, 1965. xiv + 219 pp.

Prose and verse of Spain and Spanish America from the fourteenth to the twentieth century.

539. Cohen, J. M., ed. *The Penguin Book of Spanish Verse.* Baltimore: Penguin Books, 1956. xxxvi + 442 pp.

Original Spanish with prose translations from earliest to contemporary poetry.

540. Espína García, Antonio, ed. *Las mejores escenas del teatro español e hispanoamericano* (*desde sus orígenes hasta la época actual*). Madrid: Aguilar, 1959. 1,172 pp.

Works of 66 Spanish and eight Spanish American playwrights, with introductions to each.

541. Onís, Federico de, ed. *Antología de la poesía española e hispanoamericana* (*1882–1932*). Reprint. New York: Las Americas, 1961 (1934). xxxvi + 1,212 pp.

A classic collection which contains a wealth of biobibliographic information.

542. Sanjuán, Pilar A. *El ensayo hispánico: Estudio y antología.* Madrid: Gredos, 1954. 412 pp.

Anthology as well as study of Spanish and Spanish American essayists. Good bibliography for each author as well as a general bibliography. Factual errors and poor introduction.

543. Valverde, José M., ed. *Antología de la poesía española e hispanoamericana.* Mexico: Renacimiento, 1962. 2 vols.

From the tenth century to the present.

Spain

General

544. Del Río, Angel, and Emilia A. de Del Río, eds. *Antología general de la literatura española.* 2d ed. New York: Holt, Rinehart & Winston, 1960 (1954). 2 vols.

Excellent anthology from origins to the Civil War.

545. Díaz-Plaja, Guillermo, ed. *Antología mayor de la literatura española.* Madrid: Labor, 1958–62. 4 vols.

From beginnings of Spanish literature (Seneca) through the nineteenth century.

546. ———. *Tesoro breve de las letras hispánicas.* Madrid: Magisterio Español, 1968–.

Fifteen volumes planned; from *jarchas* to contemporary writers.

547. Franco, Dolores, ed. *España como preocupación.* 2d ed. Madrid: Guadarrama, 1960 (1944). 570 pp.

Very good headnotes. Selections from essayists of the seventeenth to the twentieth century. Living essayists are excluded.

548. García Mercadal, José, ed. *Antología de humoristas españoles del siglo I al XX.* 2d ed. Madrid: Aguilar, 1961 (1956). 1,773 pp.

Biographical introduction to each author.

549. Pattison, Walter T., and Donald W. Bleznick, eds. *Representative Spanish Authors.* 3d ed. New York: Oxford University Press, 1971 (1942). 2 vols.

From the *jarchas* to the late 1950s. Critical and historical essays and headnotes on the various literary schools and many authors. Abundant footnotes and extensive vocabulary.

550. Romera-Navarro, Miguel, ed. *Antología de la literatura española desde los orígenes hasta principios del siglo XIX.* Boston: D. C. Heath & Co., 1933. xi + 425 pp.

Still useful. From the *Cantar de Mio Cid* to *El sí de las niñas.* Good notes and glossary.

Period

551. Díaz-Plaja, Fernando, ed. *Antología del romanticismo español.* 2d ed. New York: McGraw-Hill Book Co., 1968 (1959). 252 pp.

Selections chosen to illustrate the idea and major themes of romanticism.

552. Ford, Jeremiah D. M. *Old Spanish Readings.* 2d ed. Boston: Ginn & Co., 1911 (1906). 312 pp.

Detailed analysis of some early Spanish writings. Etymological vocabulary.

553. Fotitch, Tatiana, ed. *An Anthology of Old Spanish.* Washington, D.C.: Catholic University of America Press, 1962. vii + 253 pp.

From oldest documents to the fifteenth century. Texts for study of Vulgar Latin.

554. Gifford, D. J., and F. W. Hodcroft, eds. *Textos lingüísticos del medioevo español.* Oxford: Dolphin, 1959. 283 pp.

Texts from different provinces of Spain. Vocabulary and glossary.

555. Kohler, Eugene, ed. *Antología de la literatura española de la Edad Media (1140–1500).* Paris: C. Klincksieck, 1957. 418 pp.

Contains glossary and preliminary notes to various sections.

556. Romero, Mariana, ed. *Paisaje y literatura de España: Antología de los escritores del 98.* Madrid: Tecnos, 1957. 430 pp.

Seven writers treating the Spanish landscape.

Genres

Prose

557. Arco, Juan del, ed. *Novelistas españoles contemporáneos.* Madrid: Aldecoa, 1944. 439 pp.

Selections from works written between the years 1893 and 1943. Major authors from Valle-Inclán to Cela. Biographical data and bibliographies.

558. Blecua, José Manuel, ed. *Escritores costumbristas.* Zaragoza: Ebro, 1960. 133 pp.

Selections by Larra, Mesonero Romanos, and Estébanez Calderón.

559. Bleznick, Donald W., ed. *El ensayo español del siglo veinte.* New York: Ronald Press, 1964. 294 pp.

From Unamuno to Julián Marías. Brief history of the Spanish essay from the sixteenth century and headnotes on each of ten essayists represented.

560. Buendía, Felicidad, ed. *Antología de la novela histórica española (1834–1844).* Madrid: Aguilar, 1963. 1,803 pp.

Biobibliographical data are included.

561. Correa Calderón, E., ed. *Costumbristas españoles.* Madrid: Aguilar, 1950. 2 vols.

An extensive collection with introduction.

562. Del Río, Angel, and M. J. Benardete, eds. *El conceptocontemporáneo de España.* Buenos Aires: Losada, 1946. 741 pp.

Very good anthology and headnotes. Includes essays written between 1895 and 1931. The long introduction is a mine of information on the origins and development of the Spanish essay.

563. Díaz-Plaja, Guillermo, ed. *El poema en prosa en España: Estudio crítico y antología.* Barcelona: G. Gili, 1956. 404 pp.

Lengthy introduction. Eighty-four authors from modernism to mid-twentieth century.

564. Entrambasaguas, Joaquín de, and María del Pilar Palomo, eds. *Las mejores novelas contemporáneas.* 2d ed. Barcelona: Planeta, 1962–63 (1957). 9 vols.

Five novels in each volume. Covers the years 1895–1939. Bibliographies of novels and authors as well as general bibliographies.

565. García Pavón, Francisco, ed. *Antología de cuentistas españoles contemporáneos (1939–1966).* 2d ed. Madrid: Gredos, 1966 (1959). 454 pp.

Some 50 authors are represented. Biobibliographic headnotes.

566. Herrero García, Miguel, ed. *Cuentos de los siglos XVI y XVII.* Madrid: Instituto-Escuela Junta para Ampliación de Estudios, 1926. 285 pp.

Twenty-two *cuentistas* from Guevara to Francisco Santos.

567. Maeztu, María de, ed. *Antología siglo XX: Prosistas españoles; semblanzas y comentarios.* 2d ed. Madrid: Espasa-Calpe, 1964 (1943). 248 pp.

First half contains essays dealing with the *Quijote.* Good anthology and cogent *semblanzas.*

568. Menéndez Pidal, Ramón, ed. *Antología de prosistas españoles.* 7th ed. Buenos Aires and Mexico: Espasa-Calpe, 1956 (1899). 303 pp.

Biographical notes and comments on works. From Alfonso "el Sabio" to the beginning of the nineteenth century.

569. Sáinz de Robles, Federico, ed. *La novela corta española: Promoción de "El cuento semanal" (1901–1920).* Madrid: Aguilar, 1959. 1,804 pp.

Introduction treats the novel of the early twentieth century. Brief sketch of each author.

570. Valbuena Prat, Angel, ed. *La novela picaresca española.* Madrid: Aguilar, 1946. 2,051 pp.

Lengthy study of picaresque novel and texts of many important picaresque novels. Useful indexes.

Theater

571. Alpern, Hymen, José Martel, and Leonard Mades, eds. *Diez comedias del Siglo de Oro.* 2d ed. New York: Harper & Row, 1968 (1939). xxx + 865 pp.

Many helpful features such as bibliographies, metrical schemes, and extensive notes.

572. Brett, Lewis E., ed. *Nineteenth-Century Spanish Plays.* New York: Appleton-Century, 1935. ix + 889 pp.

Fifteen plays by as many playwrights from Moratín to Benavente.

573. Díaz-Plaja, Fernando, ed. *Teatro español: Antología (1939–1958).* Madrid: Alfil, 1958. 314 pp.

Some 15 writers are represented.

574. González Ruiz, Nicolás, ed. *Piezas maestras del teatro teológico español.* 2d ed. Madrid: Editorial Católica, 1963 (1958). lxxi + 923 pp.

Autos sacramentales and *comedias* written primarily by major figures of the Golden Age.

575. Lázaro Carreter, Fernando, ed. *Teatro medieval.* 2d ed. Valencia: Editorial Castalia, 1965 (1958). 285 pp.

Contains a good introduction to the medieval theater.

576. Sáinz de Robles, Federico, ed. *Teatro español.* Madrid: Aguilar, 1951–. Published annually.

Selection of the five best plays of each theatrical season since 1949–50. Includes comments by critics and authors.

577. ———. *El teatro español: Historia y antología desde el siglo XIV al XIX.* Madrid: Aguilar, 1942–43. 7 vols.

Also contains studies of periods and authors as well as notes and bibliographies.

578. Valencia, Antonio, ed. *El género chico: Antología de textos completos.* Madrid: Taurus, 1962. 619 pp.

Fifteen plays of the nineteenth century.

Poetry

579. Alonso, Dámaso, ed. *Poesía de la Edad Media y poesía de tipo tradicional.* 2d ed. Buenos Aires: Losada, 1942 (1935). 558 pp.

From the *Cid* to 1550.

580. Alonso, Dámaso, and José Manuel Blecua, eds. *Antología de la poesía española: Lírica de tipo tradicional.* 2d ed. Madrid: Gredos, 1964 (1956). lxxxvi + 263 pp.

Basic scholarly anthology of traditional poetry. Good introduction and notes.

581. Altolaguirre, Manuel, ed. *Antología de la poesía romántica española.* Buenos Aires: Espasa-Calpe Argentina, 1954. 210 pp.

Twenty-one poets from Arjona to Rosalía de Castro. Brief biographies.

582. Barnstone, Willis, ed. *Spanish Poetry: From Its Beginnings through the Nineteenth Century.* New York: Oxford University Press, 1970. xxi + 526 pp.

Introduction, headnotes, notes, and bibliography. Many poets are well represented.

583. Blecua, José M., ed. *Floresta de lírica española.* 1st reprinting of 2d ed. Madrid: Gredos, 1968 (1957). 2 vols.

Volume 1 extends from *jarchas* to San Juan, and volume 2 from the eighteenth century to Miguel Hernández and José Luis Hidalgo.

584. Buchanan, Milton A., ed. *Spanish Poetry of the Golden Age.* Toronto: University of Toronto Press, 1942. 148 pp.

Notes to each selection. Covers years 1400–1650.

585. Cano, José Luis, ed. *Antología de la nueva poesía española.* 3d ed. Madrid: Gredos, 1968 (1958). 438 pp.

An extensive collection from Miguel Hernández to the latest poets, with biobibliographic information on each.

586. Correa, Gustavo, ed. *Poesía española del siglo veinte.* New York: Appleton-Century-Crofts, 1972. 613 pp.

Contains a useful introduction to modern Spanish poetry, beginning with the second half of the nineteenth century. From Unamuno to the most recent poets, each one well represented by at least several selections. Biobibliographic introduction to each poet and an extensive bibliography.

587. Cossío, José María de, ed. *Los toros en la poesía castellana.* Madrid: Compañía Ibero-Americana de Publicaciones, 1931. 2 vols.

Study and anthology from the Middle Ages to the twentieth century.

588. Cueto, Leopoldo Augusto de, ed. *Poetas líricos del siglo XVIII.* Vols. 61, 63, 67 of *Biblioteca de autores españoles.* Madrid: Atlas, 1952. 3 vols.

Still the only useful and complete source of poetic texts for the eighteenth century.

589. Diego, Gerardo, ed. *Poesía española contemporánea.* 4th ed. Madrid: Taurus Ediciones, 1968 (1932). 673 pp.

An influential anthology that represents some 30 poets.

590. Fitzmaurice-Kelly, James, and J. B. Trend, eds. *The Oxford Book of Spanish Verse.* 2d ed. Oxford: Clarendon Press, 1940 (1913). xxxix + 522 pp.

Poetry from the thirteenth to the twentieth century.

591. Foulché-Delbosc, Raymond, ed. *Cancionero castellano del siglo XV.* Vols. 19 and 22 of *Nueva biblioteca de autores españoles.* Madrid: Casa Editorial Bailly-Baillière, 1912–15. 2 vols.

Very informative introduction to each author.

592. Landínez, Luis, ed. *Antología de la poesía española en la Edad Media* (*castellana, catalana y gallega*). Barcelona: Iberia, 1948. 178 pp.

Notes include bibliography.

593. Marín, Diego, ed. *Poesía española: Siglos XV al XX.* Chapel Hill, N.C.: Estudios de Hispanófila, 1971. 537 pp. Revised and enlarged edition of *Lira española* (Toronto: Ryerson Press, 1954).

Good selection. Introduction, extensive notes (in English), and vocabulary.

594. Menéndez Pelayo, Marcelino, ed. *Antología de poetas líricos castellanos desde la formación del idioma hasta nuestros días.* Madrid: Libería de Prelado Páez, 1890–1914. 13 vols.

595. Menéndez Pidal, Ramón, ed. *Flor nueva de romances viejos.* 2d ed. Madrid: Espasa-Calpe, 1943 (1928). 316 pp.

Romances on a variety of subjects by the foremost authority in the field.

596. ⸻. *Reliquias de la poesía épica española.* Madrid: Espasa-Calpe, 1951. lxxviii + 293 pp.

Very informative introduction on various aspects of the medieval epic.

597. Menéndez Pidal, Ramón, and María Goyri, eds. *Romancero tradicional de las lenguas hispánicas* (*español-portugués-catalán-sefardí*). Madrid: Gredos, 1953. 2 vols.

The *romancero* and its relationship to Moorish-Christian legends.

598. Peers, E. Allison, ed. *A Critical Anthology of Spanish Verse.* Liverpool: University Press, 1948. 741 pp.

Useful for its analyses of many poems by Spain's finest poets.

599. Perry, Janet, ed. *The Heath Anthology of Spanish Poetry.* Boston: D. C. Heath & Co., 1953. 468 pp.

Good introduction on meter in Spanish poetry.

600. Rivers, Elias, ed. *Renaissance and Baroque Poetry of Spain.* Reprint. New York: Charles Scribner's Sons, 1973 (1966). 351 pp.

Nearly 200 poems from the works of 25 poets together with prose translations.

601. Terry, Arthur, ed. *An Anthology of Spanish Poetry, 1500–1700.* Oxford: Pergamon Press, 1965. 2 vols.

Introduction, headnotes, and many footnotes explicating the poetry covered.

Spanish America

General

602. Anderson-Imbert, Enrique, and Eugenio Florit, eds. *Literatura hispanoamericana: Antología e introducción histórica.* 2d ed. New York: Holt, Rinehart & Winston, 1970 (1960). 2 vols.

Works of all epochs with introductory comments.

603. Caracciolo-Trejo, Enrique, ed. *The Penguin Book of Latin American Verse.* Harmondsworth and Baltimore: Penguin Books, 1971. xlv + 425 pp.

Includes the best nineteenth- and twentieth-century poets of practically every Latin American country. Contains English prose translations of every poem, an introduction, very brief biobibliographic notes, and an explanatory guide to movements in Latin American poetry.

604. Castillo, Homero, ed. *Antología de poetas modernistas hispanoamericanos.* Englewood Cliffs, N.J.: Prentice-Hall, 1972. 505 pp.

Contains brief introduction; bibliographies; vocabulary; and glossary of terms, places, historical and mythological characters, and so forth.

Craig. *Modernist Trend in Spanish-American Poetry.* See no. 529.

605. Englekirk, John, Irving Leonard, John Reid, and John Crow, eds. *An Anthology of Spanish American Literature.* 3d ed. New York: Appleton-Century-Crofts, 1968 (1946). xiv + 772 pp.

From Hernán Cortés to the present day. Very few excerpts from novels and plays. This is a companion volume to *An Outline History of Spanish American Literature* (see no. 348).

606. Flores, Angel, ed. *The Literature of Spanish America: A Critical Anthology.* New York: Las Americas, 1966–67. 4 vols.

From the colonial period to the 1960s. Texts in Spanish; notes and bibliography in English.

607. Florit, Eugenio, and José Olivio Jiménez, eds. *La poesía hispanoamericana desde el modernismo.* New York: Appleton-Century-Crofts, 1968. xvi + 482 pp.

Selections of poetry from 72 different poets arranged in five major sections: modernism, postmodernism, vanguardism, postvanguardism, and recent tendencies. Biographical sketches of each author and selected critical bibliography.

608. García Prada, Carlos, ed. *Poetas modernistas hispanoamericanos.* Madrid: Cultura Hispánica, 1956. 355 pp.

Introductory study, critical and bibliographic notes, and selections from 15 poets.

609. Gómez-Gil, Orlando, ed. *Literatura hispanoamericana: Antología crítica.* New York: Holt, Rinehart & Winston, 1972. 2 vols.

From pre-Hispanic period to present. All genres represented except the novel.

610. Jiménez, José Olivio, ed. *Antología de la poesía hispanoamericana contemporánea, 1914–1970.* Madrid: Alianza Editorial, 1971. 508 pp.

Numerous selections taken from 37 well-known poets.

611. Jones, Willis Knapp, ed. *Antología del teatro hispanoamericano.* Mexico: Ediciones de Andrea, 1958. 254 pp.

Modern dramatists as well as Sor Juana Inés de la Cruz.

612. Latcham, Ricardo, ed. *Antología del cuento hispanoamericano contemporáneo, 1910–1956.* 2d ed. Santiago de Chile: Zig-Zag, 1962 (1958). 450 pp.

Sixty-six authors of every Spanish American country are included.

613. Leal, Luis, and Frank Dauster, eds. *Literatura de Hispanoamérica.* New York: Harcourt, Brace & World, 1970. 560 pp.

From pre-Columbian literature to the contemporary period. Includes complete works of all genres except the novel. Introduction, bibliographic information on authors, and notes.

614. Mejía Sánchez, Ernesto, and Pedro Guillén, eds. *El ensayo actual latinoamericano.* Mexico: Ediciones de Andrea, 1971. 288 pp.

Contemporary essayists from 21 countries, including such authors as Arciniegas, Mañach, Arévalo, Pedro Henríquez Ureña, Zum Felde, and Picón Salas.

615. Menéndez y Pelayo, Marcelino, ed. *Antología de poetas* *hispanoamericanos.* 2d ed. Madrid: Real Academia Española, 1927–28 (1893–95). 4 vols.

Lengthy introductory study. Includes writers from the colonial period to the late nineteenth century.

616. Menton, Seymour, ed. *El cuento hispanoamericano: Antología crítico-histórica.* 3d ed. Mexico: Fondo de Cultura Económica, 1970 (1964), 2 vols.

Includes the best short-story writers from romanticism to the "boom" decade (1960–70). Studies on each story and bibliography on the short story (general and by countries).

617. Reyes Nevárez, Salvador, ed. *Novelas selectas de Hispano-América, siglo XIX.* Mexico: Labor Mexicana, 1959. 2 vols.

Thirteen novels from various countries.

618. Ripoll, Carlos, ed. *Conciencia intelectual de América: Antología del ensayo hispanoamericano (1836–1959).* New York: Las Americas, 1966. 463 pp.

General introduction, headnotes, and bibliography for each of the ten essayists included.

619. Rodríguez Sardiñas, Orlando, and Carlos Miguel Suárez Radillo, eds. *Teatro contemporáneo hispanoamericano.* Madrid: Escelicer, 1971. 2 vols.

Country-by-country anthology containing mostly social drama.

620. Silva Castro, Raúl, ed. *Antología crítica del modernismo hispanoamericano.* New York: Las Americas, 1963. 376 pp.

Selections from 43 *modernista* poets that include such precursors as Rubén Darío. One critical biographical paragraph for each writer represented.

621. Solórzano, Carlos, ed. *El teatro actual latinoamericano.* Mexico: Ediciones de Andrea, 1972. 338 pp.

Eight plays by as many playwrights. Some of the dramatists represented are Carlos Gorostiza (Argentina), Enrique Buenaventura (Colombia), Isidora Aguirre (Chile), and Demetrio Aguilera Malta (Ecuador).

622. ———. *El teatro hispanoamericano contemporáneo.* Mexico: Fondo de Cultura Económica, 1964. 2 vols.

Plays by 14 dramatists from as many countries. Solórzano, Benedetti, Salazar Bondy, Marqués, and Aguilera Malta are among those included.

National (alphabetized by country)

Argentina

623. Berenguer Carisomo, Arturo, ed. *Antología argentina contemporánea.* Buenos Aires: Huemul, 1970. 250 pp.

Verse and prose of three literary movements of this century: *postmodernista,* generation of 1922 (*vanguardistas*), and generation of 1940. Introduction, biobibliographic notes, textual commentaries, and glossary.

624. ———. *Teatro argentino contemporáneo.* Madrid: Aguilar, 1962. 475 pp.

Contains introductory study and notes on the dramatists and their works. Samuel Eichelbaum and Nalé Roxlo are among the seven playwrights included.

625. Fernández Moreno, César, and Horacio Jorge Becco, eds. *Antología lineal de la poesía argentina.* Madrid: Gredos, 1968. 384 pp.

From the colonial to the contemporary period. Bibliography.

626. Ghiano, Juan, ed. *Poesía argentina del siglo XX.* Mexico: Fondo de Cultura Económica, 1957. 285 pp.

Ninety-three poets are represented.

627. Henríquez Ureña, Pedro, and Jorge Luis Borges, eds. *Antología clásica de la literatura argentina.* Buenos Aires: A. Kapelusz, 1937. 445 pp.

Thirty-six authors from the sixteenth century to the twentieth. Each selection is preceded by a biobibliographic sketch.

628. Ordaz, Luis, ed. *Breve historia del teatro argentino.* Buenos Aires: Editorial Universitaria de Buenos Aires, 1962–66. 8 vols.

Selections from more than 20 playwrights of the nineteenth and twentieth centuries. Introductions to the theater of each period.

629. Yahni, Roberto, ed. *70 años de narrativa argentina: 1900–1970.* Madrid: Alianza Editorial, 1970. 212 pp.

Lugones, Güiraldes, Quiroga, Martínez Estrada, Borges, Mallea, and Cortázar are among the 18 authors included. Contains a brief introduction and biobibliographic notes.

Bolivia

630. Baptista Gumuncio, Mariano, ed. *Narradores bolivianos.* Caracas: Monte Avila, 1969. 256 pp.

Fourteen authors are included, most of whom started to publish around 1950.

631. Bedregal, Yolando, ed. *Poesía de Bolivia: De la época precolombina al modernismo.* Buenos Aires: Editorial Universitaria, 1964. 123 pp.

General introduction. Most selections are from nineteenth-century poets. Brief biographical notes.

632. Díaz Machicao, Porfirio, ed. *Prosa y verso de Bolivia.* La Paz: Los Amigos del Libro, 1966–68. 4 vols.

Most of the writers are of the twentieth century. Includes brief biobibliographic sketches for all authors represented.

633. Quirós, Juan, ed. *Indice de la poesía boliviana contemporánea.* La Paz: Juventud, 1964. 440 pp.

An extensive collection of Bolivian poets with concise biobibliographic and critical comments for each writer.

634. Soriano Badani, Armando, ed. *El cuento boliviano* (*1900–1937*). Buenos Aires: Editorial Universitaria, 1964. 160 pp.

Fourteen writers are represented. General introduction and brief biographical note for each author.

635. Viscarra Fabre, Guillermo, ed. *Poetas nuevos de Bolivia.* La Paz: Ministerio de Relaciones Exteriores, 1941. 286 pp.

Biographies and works of 25 poets.

Chile

636. Bunster, César, Julio Durán Cerda, Pedro Lastra, and Benjamín Rojas Piña, eds. *Antología del cuento chileno.* 2d ed. Santiago: Editorial Universitaria, Instituto de Literatura Chilena, 1965 (1963). 631 pp.

Extensive anthology of nineteenth- and twentieth-century Chilean short fiction. Biobibliographic data for each author.

637. Durán Cerda, Julio, ed. *Panorama del teatro chileno, 1842–1959.* Santiago: Editorial del Pacífico, 1959. 371 pp.

Contains introductory study to and bibliography of the Chilean theater.

638. Montes, Hugo, and Julio Orlandi, eds. *Historia y antología de la literatura chilena.* 7th ed. Santiago: Editorial del Pacífico, 1965. 682 pp.

Manual of Chilean literature from Valdivia's letters to Neruda. The second part, divided by generations, is devoted to fiction, the third to poetry, the fourth to criticism and the essay, and the fifth to theater.

639. Scarpa Roque, Esteban, and Hugo Montes, eds. *Antología de la poesía chilena contemporánea.* Madrid: Gredos, 1968. 372 pp.
Poetry since 1920 of 26 poets. Brief biobibliography for each author.

640. Silva Castro, Raúl, ed. *Antología general de la poesía chilena.* Santiago: Zig-Zag, 1959. 433 pp.
The best-known poems of all Chilean poets who were dead at the time of publication. Brief biobibliography for each poet.

641. *Teatro chileno contemporáneo.* Madrid: Aguilar, 1970. 498 pp.
Egon Wolff, Luis Alberto Heiremans, and Sergio Vodanovic are among the six dramatists represented.

642. Yáñez, María Flora, ed. *Antología del cuento chileno moderno.* 2d ed. Santiago: Editorial del Pacífico, 1965 (1958). 317 pp.
Chilean short fiction since 1938.

Colombia

643. Arango, Daniel, ed. *Las mejores poesías colombianas.* Bogota: Compañía Grancolombiana de Ediciones, 1959. 163 pp.
Twenty-seven poets from the time of the conquest to the middle of the twentieth century. Rafael Pombo, José Asunción Silva, Guillermo Valencia, Eduardo Castillo, Porfirio Barba-Jacob, and Luis Carlos López are among the best represented. Andrés Holguín provides a brief introduction to Colombian literature.

644. Arbeláez, Fernando, ed. *Panorama de la nueva poesía colombiana.* Bogota: Ministerio de Educación, Imprenta Nacional, 1964. 548 pp.
Chronological arrangement of poets. Lacks biobibliographic data.

645. Echeverría Mejía, Oscar, and Alfonso Bonella-Narr, eds. *Veintiún años de poesía colombiana (1942–1963).* Bogota: Stella, 1964. 404 pp.
Selections from 131 poets.

646. Holguín, Andrés, ed. *Los mejores cuentos colombianos.* Bogota: Compañía Grancolombiana de Ediciones, 1959. 108 pp.
Twelve short stories by as many writers from Jesús del Corral to Eduardo Caballero Calderón. No introduction or bibliography.

647. López Narváez, Carlos, ed. *Poemas de Colombia.* Medellín: Bedout, 1959. 623 pp.

An extensive anthology sponsored by the Colombian Academy. Prologue and epilogue by Félix Restrepo.

Costa Rica

648. Bonilla, Abelardo, ed. *Historia y antología de la literatura costarricense.* San José: Trejes, 1957–61. 2 vols.

Extensive treatment from colonial era to the 1950s. Lacks bibliography.

649. Ferrero, Luis, ed. *Ensayistas costarricenses.* San José: Librería Antonio Lehmann, 1971. 358 pp.

History and anthology of the Costa Rican essay. Also contains a bibliography of individual essayists.

650. Menton, Seymour, ed. *El cuento costarricense.* Mexico: Ediciones de Andrea, 1964. 184 pp.

Only comprehensive presentation of the Costa Rican short story. Includes critical study, lengthy bibliography, and anthology of 24 short stories by 22 authors.

651. Sotela, Rogelio, ed. *Escritores de Costa Rica.* San José: Imprenta Lehmann, 1942. 885 pp.

Brief selections of many authors from the colonial period to the twentieth century.

Cuba

652. Bueno, Salvador, ed. *Antología del cuento en Cuba (1902–1952).* Havana: Ediciones de Cincuentenario, Dirección de Cultura del Ministerio de Educación, 1953. 339 pp.

Short stories by 42 writers, with brief biographies.

653. Caballero Bonald, José Manuel, ed. *Narrativa cubana de la revolución.* Madrid: Alianza Editorial, 1968. 258 pp.

Twenty-four representative contemporary writers from Carpentier to Arenas. Biobibliographic data on each author.

654. Fornet, Ambrosio, ed. *Antología del cuento cubano contemporáneo.* Mexico: Ediciones Era, 1967. 241 pp.

Jesús Castellanos, Cabrera Infante, and Humberto Arenal are among the authors represented. Introduction and comments on each author are included.

655. García Vega, Lorenzo, ed. *Antología de la novela en Cuba.* Havana: Ministerio de Educación, 1960. 508 pp.

Selections of 10 to 50 pages from 22 Cuban novelists, beginning with Cirilo Villaverde and extending through Alejo Carpentier to four younger authors, for example, Lezama Lima. Biographical data and some critical comments.

656. Lezama Lima, José, ed. *Antología de la poesía cubana.* Havana: Consejo Nacional de Cultura, 1965. 3 vols.

Copious anthology of Cuban poetry from its beginnings to the late nineteenth century. Introduction, commentaries, and bibliographies.

657. Martí de Cid, Dolores, ed. *Teatro cubano contemporáneo.* 2d ed. Madrid: Aguilar, 1962. 448 pp.

Six plays. Also contains an essay on the Cuban theater before Castro by José Cid Pérez.

Dominican Republic

658. *Antología de la literatura dominicana.* Santiago, Dominican Republic: Edición del Gobierno Dominicano, 1944. 2 vols.

Volume 1 contains poetry, and volume 2 includes prose. A comprehensive anthology.

659. Cartegena, Aída, ed. *Narradores dominicanos.* Caracas: Monte Avila, 1969. 153 pp.

Includes 11 authors, of whom nine belong to the post-Trujillo era.

660. Fernández Spencer, Antonio, ed. *Nueva poesía dominicana.* Madrid: Cultura Hispánica, 1953. 344 pp.

Large number of compositions by nine poets who represent the period 1916–47.

Ecuador

661. Carrión, Benjamín, ed. *El nuevo relato ecuatoriano.* 2d ed. Quito: Casa de la Cultura Ecuatoriana, 1958 (1950–51). 1,124 pp.

Extensive collection of Ecuadorian prose fiction with a long but interesting personal criticism by the editor which includes comparisons with other notable American and European literary figures.

662. Medina Cifuentes, Enrique, ed. *Poetas del Ecuador.* Quito: Ediciones Medina, 1966. 197 pp.

One hundred poets are represented in alphabetical order, with no information given on them.

663. Pesantez Rodas, Rodrigo, ed. *La nueva literatura ecuatoriana.* Vol. 1, *Poesía.* Guayaquil: Universidad de Guayaquil, 1966. 219 pp.

Contemporary poets of Ecuador. Apparently first of a series of anthologies which will cover all genres. Brief biographies of each poet.

El Salvador

664. Barba Salinas, Manuel, ed. *Antología del cuento salvadoreño (1880–1955)*. San Salvador: Ministerio de Cultura, 1959. 512 pp.

Twenty-eight authors are represented, with brief biographical notes on each.

665. Cea, José Roberto, ed. *Antología general de la poesía salvadoreña*. San Salvador: Editorial Universitaria, 1971. 482 pp.

Chronological arrangement, beginning with Francisco Gavidia. Concise general introduction and basic biobibliographies.

666. Gallagher, Jack, ed. and trans. *Modern Short Stories of El Salvador*. San Salvador: Ministerio de Educación, 1966. 201 pp.

El Salvador's nine most important short-story writers from Salarrué to Menéndez Leal are represented, with interesting and typically Salvadoran stories.

Guatemala

667. Echeverría, B., and R. Amílcar, eds. *Antología de la literatura guatemalteca: Prosa y verso, leyenda, tradición, novela, cuento, crónica, ensayo, picaresca, poesía*. Guatemala: Editorial Savia, 1960. 759 pp.

A broad spectrum of Guatemalan literature.

668. Lamb, Ruth, ed. *Antología del cuento guatemalteco*. Mexico: Ediciones de Andrea, 1959. 142 pp.

Contains a variety of stories and bibliography.

669. Solórzano, Carlos, ed. *Teatro guatemalteco contemporáneo*. Madrid: Aguilar, 1964. 327 pp.

Plays by Arévalo, Asturias, Marsicovétere, Galich, and Solórzano.

Honduras

670. Acosta, Oscar, ed. *Poesía hondureña de hoy*. Tegucigalpa: Nuevo Continente, 1971. 271 pp.

Includes the traditional and social poetry of 20 Honduran poets.

671. Acosta, Oscar, and Roberto Sosa, eds. *Antología del cuento hondureño*. Tegucigalpa: Universidad Nacional Autónoma de Honduras, Departamento de Extensión Universitaria, 1968. 242 pp.

First anthology of the Honduran short story, which includes 39 stories by 27 authors from Juan Ramón Molina to César Escoto (b. 1944).

672. Durón, R. E., ed. *Honduras literaria: Colección de escritos en prosa y verso, escritores en verso precedidos de apuntes biográficos.* Tegucigalpa: Ministerio de Educación Pública, 1957. 3 vols.

673. Luna Mejía, Manuel, ed. *Indice general de la poesía hondureña.* Prólogo de Eliseo Pérez Cadalso. Mexico: Editora Latinoamericana, 1961. 1,126 pp.

A comprehensive collection of selected poems by 155 Honduran poets from the early nineteenth century to 1950.

Mexico

674. Abreu Gómez, E., J. Zavala, C. López Trujillo, and A. Henestrosa, eds. *Cuatro siglos de literatura mexicana.* Mexico: Leyenda, 1946. 1,060 pp.

Broad and varied in scope, this anthology contains selections from poetry, theater, novel, and short fiction.

675. Castro Leal, Antonio, ed. *Las cien mejores poesías líricas mexicanas.* 5th ed. Mexico: Porrúa, 1961 (1914). 306 pp.

A basic anthology by a good critic.

676. ———. *La novela de la revolución mexicana.* 4th ed. Madrid-Mexico-Buenos Aires: Aguilar, 1963. 2 vols.

Contains a general introduction, a historical chronology, lists of characters and places, as well as vocabulary and bibliography for a good representation of the novel of the Mexican Revolution.

677. ———. *La novela del México colonial.* 2d ed. Mexico: Aguilar, 1965 (1964). 2 vols.

Contains an introductory study. Bibliographies and biographies of novelists are also included.

678. Leal, Luis, ed. *Antología del cuento mexicano.* Mexico: Ediciones de Andrea, 1957. 162 pp.

Mexican short stories from the *Popol Vuh* to Revueltas, Arreola, and Rulfo.

679. Martínez, José Luis, ed. *El ensayo mexicano moderno.* Mexico: Fondo de Cultura Económica, 1958. 2 vols. English version, *The Modern Mexican Essay,* translated by H. W. Hilborn (Toronto: University of Toronto Press, 1965). 524 pp.

General introduction to the essay and biobibliographies of the 56 essayists represented. The writers range from the nineteenth century to 1958.

680. Millán, María del Carmen, ed. *Poesía romántica mexicana.* Mexico: Libro Mexicano Editores, 1957. 145 pp.

Contains an introductory study and compositions of 21 poets. Also has bibliographies.

681. Monterde, Francisco, Antonio Magaña Esquivel, and Celestino Gorostiza, eds. *Teatro mexicano del siglo XX.* Mexico: Fondo de Cultura Económica, 1956–70. Vols. 1–3, 1956; vols. 4–5, 1970.

Biographies and works of many dramatists up to the 1960s.

682. Paz, Octavio, et al., eds. *Poesía en movimiento: México, 1915–1966.* Prologue by Octavio Paz. Mexico: Siglo XXI Editores, 1966. 476 pp.

Twentieth-century Mexican poetry represented with no apparent plan of organization.

683. Rojas Garcidueñas, José, ed. *Autos y coloquios del siglo XVI.* Mexico: Universidad Nacional Autónoma de México, 1939. xxiv + 173 pp.

Introduction and four plays.

Nicaragua

684. *Antología del cuento nicaragüense.* Managua: Ediciones del Club del Libro Nicaragüense, 1957. 278 pp.

Sixteen writers of the twentieth century are represented, each by three short stories. Short biobibliographic introductions to each writer. Also includes a 10-page glossary of *nicaraguanismos*.

685. Gutiérrez, Ernesto, and José Reyes Monterrey, eds. *Poesía nicaragüense postdariana.* León: Universidad Nacional Autónoma de Nicaragua, 1967. 250 pp.

Contains compositions of 30 poets arranged more or less by generation.

686. Sánchez, María Teresa, ed. *Poesía nicaragüense: Antología.* Managua: Nuevos Horizontes, 1948. 320 pp.

About 180 poets, born as far back as 1779, are represented, each with one composition in most cases.

Panama

687. Jaramillo Levi, Enrique, ed. *Antología crítica de la joven narrativa panameña.* Mexico: Federación Editorial Mexicana, 1971. 285 pp.

Includes 45 short stories of 11 authors, with comments on most of the stories.

688. Miró, Rodrigo, ed. *Cien años de poesía en Panamá (1852–1952).* Panama: Imprenta Nacional, 1953. xx + 351 pp.

Panorama of the history of poetry in Panama from 1852 to 1952. A brief introduction outlines a view of the period concerned and defines the various movements into which the selections are grouped: romantics, *modernistas,* first and second generations of the Republic, the "new poetry," and the latest arrivals. Biobibliographic data.

689. ———. *El cuento en Panamá.* Panama: Imprenta de la Academia, 1950. 208 pp.

Contains a general introduction by the editor and short stories of 22 authors since the seventeenth century, beginning with Gonzalo Fernández de Oviedo. Biobibliographic data on each author and general bibliography of the short story and the novel in Panama.

690. Sánchez, Agustín del, ed. *Nueva poesía panameña.* Madrid: Cultura Hispánica, 1954. 430 pp.

Introductory study and biobibliographic data of 36 poets represented.

Paraguay

691. Pérez-Maricevich, Francisco, ed. *Breve antología del cuento paraguayo.* Asunción: Ediciones Comuneros, 1969. 200 pp.

Of the seven authors, Roa Bastos is represented by four stories, and Gabriel Casaccia and Josefina Plá by two each. Contains a 10-page introduction.

692. Plá, Josefina. *Antología de la poesía paraguaya.* Madrid: Imprenta Nacional del Estado, 1966. 45 pp.

A brief sampling by a creative writer and prolific critic.

693. Vallejos, Roque, ed. *Antología crítica de la poesía paraguaya contemporánea.* Asunción: Editorial Don Bosco, 1968. 195 pp.

Selections and presentation of outstanding Paraguayan poets from 1940 on. Contains bibliography.

Peru

694. Escobar, Alberto, ed. *Antología de la poesía peruana.* Lima: Nuevo Mundo, 1965. 219 pp.

Contains history of Peruvian poetry, biobibliographic data, and stylistic study.

695. ———. *El cuento peruano (1825–1925).* Buenos Aires: Editorial Universitaria, 1964. 120 pp.

Twelve writers are represented. Brief general introduction and biographical note for each writer included.

696. ———. *La narración en el Perú: Estudio preliminar, antología.* 2d ed. Lima: Mejía Baca, 1960 (1956). xxxvi + 512 pp.

Informative, historically arranged introduction. Good selection of Peruvian stories showing certain constants that lend a continuity to the Peruvian narrative.

697. Hesse Murga, José, ed. *Teatro peruano contemporáneo.* 2d ed. Madrid: Aguilar, 1963 (1959). 409 pp.

Five dramatists are represented: Percy Gibson Parra, Juan Ríos, Bernardo Roca Rey, Sebastián Salazar Bondy, and Enrique Solari Swayne.

698. Oquendo, Abelardo, ed. *Narrativa peruana, 1950–1970.* Madrid: Alianza Editorial, 1973. 308 pp.

Among the 14 novelists represented are such writers as Vargas Llosa, C. F. Zavaleta, Alfredo Bryce Echenique, Julio Ortega, and Luis Loayza. A 38-page introductory section contains the responses of each author to seven questions on the current Peruvian narrative and aspects of the author's literary life.

699. Oviedo, José Miguel, ed. *Narradores peruanos.* Caracas: Monte Avila, 1968. 278 pp.

Twelve twentieth-century Peruvian writers of fiction are represented, mostly by one story except for the four most "important" authors (Alegría, Arguedas, Ribeyro, and Vargas Llosa), who are represented by two stories each. Oviedo provides an introduction to contemporary Peruvian short fiction.

Puerto Rico

700. Arce de Vázquez, Margot, Laura Gallego, and Luis de Arrigoitia, eds. *Lecturas puertorriqueñas: Poesía.* Sharon, Conn.: Troutman Press, 1968. 445 pp.

Includes poets from Manuel Alonso to the 1960s. Contains critical annotations and bibliography.

701. Marqués, René, ed. *Cuentos puertorriqueños de hoy.* Mexico: Club del Libro de Puerto Rico, 1959. 288 pp.

Short-story writers who belong to the generation of 1940. Includes notes in which each author explains his concept of his story included in the anthology.

702. Martínez Masdeu, Edgar, and Esther M. Melón, eds. *Literatura puertorriqueña: Antología general.* Río Piedras: Edil, 1971. 2 vols.

Volume 1 covers the nineteenth century, and volume 2 the twen-

tieth. Poets, essayists, novelists, playwrights, and short-story writers are included. Biographical sketches are provided for each author.
703. Meléndez, Concha, ed. *El arte del cuento en Puerto Rico.* New York: Las Americas, 1961. 395 pp.
   Introduction to the Puerto Rican short story and anthology from the generation of the 1930s to the present.
704. *Teatro puertorriqueño.* San Juan: Instituto de Cultura Puertorriqueña, 1959–60. 2 vols.
   Plays by M. Méndez Ballester, E. S. Belaval, F. Arriví, R. Marqués, and others.
705. Valbuena Briones, Angel, and L. Hernández Aquino, eds. *Nueva poesía de Puerto Rico.* Madrid: Cultura Hispánica, 1952. 388 pp.
   Introduction, biographies, and works of 34 poets.

Uruguay

706. Bordoli, Domingo L., ed. *Antología de la poesía uruguaya contemporánea.* Montevideo: Universidad de la República, 1966. 2 vols.
   An extensive representation of Uruguayan poetry.
707. Casal, Julio, ed. *Exposición de la poesía uruguaya: Desde su origen hasta 1940.* Montevideo: Claridad, 1940. 767 pp.
   An all-inclusive omnibus. Contains critical comments and notes.
708. Cotelo, Rubén, ed. *Narradores uruguayos.* Caracas: Monte Avila, 1969. 289 pp.
   Short stories written since 1939 by 11 writers from the twentieth century.
709. Silva Valdés, Fernán, ed. *Teatro uruguayo contemporáneo.* Madrid: Aguilar, 1960. 556 pp.
   Plays by six dramatists, including Florencio Sánchez and Vicente Martínez Cuitiño.
710. Visca, Arturo, ed. *Antología del cuento uruguayo.* Montevideo: Banda Oriental, 1968. 6 vols.
   From the end of the nineteenth century to the 1960s.

Venezuela

711. Escalona-Escalona, José Antonio, ed. *Antología general de la poesía venezolana.* Madrid: Edime, 1966. 1,051 pp.
   Contains prologue and notes by the compiler in addition to an extensive anthology.

712. Medina, José Ramón, ed. *Antología venezolana (prosa)*. Madrid: Gredos, 1962. 331 pp.
Twenty-eight writers are covered, including Rómulo Gallegos, Teresa de la Parra, Picón Salas, and Uslar Pietri. Short introduction.

713. ———. *Antología venezolana (verso)*. Madrid: Gredos, 1962. 336 pp.
Fifty-seven poets represented from the period 1918–50. Contains a short introduction.

714. Meneses, Guillermo, ed. *Antología del cuento venezolano*. Caracas: Editorial del Ministerio de Educación, 1955. 420 pp.
A personal selection from Emilio Coll to Oswaldo Trejo (b. 1928). Each story is preceded by a comment of at least 200 words.

715. Picón Salas, Mariano, ed. *Dos siglos de prosa venezolana*. Madrid: Edime, 1965. 125 pp.
Represents the various prose genres from the eighteenth century to the present. Useful preface.

716. Prisco, Rafael di, ed. *Narrativa venezolana contemporánea*. Madrid: Alianza Editorial, 1971. 210 pp.
Short stories and fragments of novels in addition to biobibliographies of authors included.

717. Suárez Radillo, Carlos Miguel, ed. *13 autores del nuevo teatro venezolano*. Caracas: Monte Avila, 1971. 535 pp.
Covers the newer theater in Venezuela. Bibliographies of the dramatists' works and a short bibliography of the contemporary theater.

10   Books on Metrics

718. Balaguer, Joaquín. *Apuntes para una historia prosódica de la métrica castellana.* Madrid: Consejo Superior de Investigaciones Científicas, 1954. 266 pp.

Studies on the poetry of Juan de Mena and other important aspects of Spanish versification.

719. Balbín, Rafael de. *Sistema de rítmica castellana.* 2d ed. Madrid: Gredos, 1968 (1963). 404 pp.

Rather complex study but valuable for its new approaches to metrics.

720. Carballo Picazo, Alfredo. *Métrica española.* Madrid: Instituto de Estudios Madrileños, 1956. 161 pp.

A clear exposition of Spanish metrics. It also contains an extensive bibliography with some annotations.

721. Clarke, Dorothy C. *A Chronological Sketch of Castilian Versification Together with a List of Its Metric Terms.* Berkeley and Los Angeles: University of California Press, 1952. 104 pp.

Based primarily on versification of lyric and epic poetry. Lengthy bibliography which serves as a supplement to the author's *Una bibliografía de versificación española* (University of California Publications in Modern Philology, vol. 20, no. 2 [1937]).

722. ———. *Morphology of Fifteenth-Century Castilian Verse.* Pittsburgh, Pa.: Duquesne University Press, 1964. 233 pp.

Based on the works of numerous fifteenth-century poets. The author studies *arte mayor,* minor meters, and the emergence of syllable count in octosyllabic verse.

723. Díez-Echarri, Emiliano. *Teorías métricas del Siglo de Oro.* Madrid: Consejo Superior de Investigaciones Científicas, 1949. 355 pp.

Passages on metrical theory of the Golden Age accompanied by the author's comments and evaluations.

724. Henríquez Ureña, Pedro. *Estudios de versificación española.* Buenos Aires: Universidad de Buenos Aires, 1961. 399 pp.

Collection of studies mainly on early Spanish poetry. Also treats Mexican poetry of the Independence period, and Ruben Darío.

725. ———. *La versificación española irregular.* 2d ed. Madrid: Centro de Estudios Históricos, 1933 (1920). viii + 369 pp.

A study of the irregular Spanish verse from the medieval period to 1920. Very informative work for any student of poetic form. Indexes of themes and authors.

726. López Estrada, Francisco. *Métrica española del siglo XX.* Madrid: Gredos, 1969. 225 pp.

Student manual that stresses twentieth-century metrics but also links it to previous poetry. Detailed study of Dámaso Alonso's ''A un río le llamaban Carlos.'' Subject and author indexes.

727. Navarro Tomás, Tomás. *Arte del verso.* Mexico: Compañía General de Ediciones, 1959. 187 pp.

Very helpful outline of meters, stanzas, and irregular forms.

728. ———. *Métrica española; reseña histórica y descriptiva.* 3d ed. Syracuse, N.Y.: Syracuse University Press, 1972 (1956). 581 pp.

Fundamental work which studies the poetic forms of each epoch, showing innovations and influences by numerous references to poets and their works.

729. Quilis, Antonio. *Métrica española.* Madrid: Alcalá, 1969. 194 pp.

A succinct, useful handbook for students. Many examples along with sample analysis.

730. Riquer, Martín de. *Resumen de versificación española.* Barcelona: Seix Barral, 1950. 86 pp.

Gives essential information on metrics.

Literature in Translation: Bibliographies

731. Engber, Marjorie, comp. *Caribbean Fiction and Poetry*. New York: Center for Inter-American Relations, 1970. 86 pp.

Includes anthologies, poetry, short stories, and novels published in the United States and Great Britain between 1900 and 1970. No annotations.

732. Hulet, Claude L. *Latin American Poetry in English Translation: A Bibliography*. Washington, D.C.: Pan American Union, 1964. xiii + 192 pp.

From the pre-Columbian period to 1963.

733. ———. *Latin American Prose in English Translation: A Bibliography*. Washington, D.C.: Pan American Union, 1964. 191 pp.

Lists translations of prose from the sixteenth century to the 1960s.

734. *Index translationum*. N.s. Paris: UNESCO, 1949–.

Annual listing of translated books. More than 70 countries are included in volume 23 (1970), published in 1972. Author index (vols. 1–6, n.s.) includes indexes of translators and publishers.

735. Leavitt, Sturgis E. *Hispano-American Literature in the United States: A Bibliography of Translations and Criticism*. Cambridge, Mass.: Harvard University Press, 1932. x + 54 pp.

This bibliography was corrected and augmented by *Hispano-American Literature in the U.S.: A Bibliography of Translations and Criticism, 1932–1934* (*with Additional Items from Earlier Years*) (Chapel Hill: University of North Carolina Press, 1935), 21 pp.

736. Levine, Susan G., comp. *Latin America: Fiction and Poetry in Translation*. New York: Center for Inter-American Relations, 1970. 72 pp.

List of anthologies (authors given) and individual works. No annotations.

737. Mitchell, Eleanor. *Spanish and Portuguese Translations of United States Books* (*1955–1962*). Washington, D.C.: Hispanic Foundation, Library of Congress, 1963. 506 pp.

Works of less than 100 pages are included only if they are plays, books of poetry, or speeches. Articles are included only if they have appeared in books.

738. **O'Brien, Robert.** *Spanish Plays in English Translation.* New York: Las Americas, 1963. 82 pp.

Brief descriptions of each author and play plus information useful to potential producers.

739. **Pane, Remigio Ugo.** *English Translations from the Spanish, 1484–1943.* New Brunswick, N.J.: Rutgers University Press, 1944. vi + 218 pp.

This work includes 2,682 items.

740. **Parks, George B., and Ruth Z. Temple, eds.** *The Literatures of the World in English Translation: A Bibliography.* New York: Frederick Ungar Publishing Co., 1970. Vol. 3, *The Romance Literatures.*

Remigio U. Pane prepared the bibliography for Spanish literature in translation (pp. 237–328), which includes books on background, literary studies, collections, and individual authors by period (medieval period, Renaissance, Golden Age, eighteenth, nineteenth, and twentieth centuries). Willis Knapp Jones prepared the bibliography for Spanish American literature (pp. 329–453), which includes background, literary studies, collections, colonial Spanish American literature, and individual authors by countries.

741. **Randall, Dale B. J.** *The Golden Tapestry: A Critical Survey of Non-Chivalric Spanish Fiction in English Translation, 1543–1657.* Durham, N.C.: Duke University Press, 1963. vii + 262 pp.

A well-organized, useful compilation.

12   Linguistics

Bibliographies

Besides the bibliographies listed below, consult the linguistics journals listed in chapter 13 (pp. 130–49). Especially useful are the bibliographies in the *Modern Language Association International Bibliography* (vol. 3), the *Nueva revista de filología hispánica,* the *Revista de filología hispánica* (1939–46), the *Revista hispánica moderna* (to vol. 34, 1966), the *Revista de filología española,* the *Romanische Bibliographie* supplements to the *Zeitschrift für romanische Philologie,* and *The Year's Work in Modern Language Studies.*

742. Alvar, Manuel. *Dialectología española.* Cuadernos Bibliográficos no. 7. Madrid: Consejo Superior de Investigaciones Científicas, 1962. 96 pp.

   Contains the following sections: general, vulgar, and regional Spanish; *mozárabe;* Spanish dialects (*leonés, extremeño, riojano, aragonés murciano, andaluz, canario*); Spanish of America; *papiamento;* Philippine Spanish; and Judeo-Spanish.

743. Avellaneda, María R. "Contribución a una bibliografía de dialectología española y especialmente hispanoamericana." *Boletín de la Real Academia Española* 46 (1966): 335–69, 525–55; 47 (1967): 125–56, 311–42.

   Arranged by author's last name. Good for early works (before 1960).

744. *Bibliographie linguistique/Linguistic Bibliography.* Utrecht and Brussels: Spectrum, 1939–. Published annually.

   Published under the auspices of the Permanent International Committee of Linguists. Includes Iberian and American Spanish in its coverage of all regions of the world.

745. *Bibliographie linguistique des années 1939–1947/Linguistic Bibliography for the Years 1939–1947.* Utrecht and Brussels: Spectrum, 1949–50. 2 vols.

   Supported by UNESCO to fill gap caused by Second World War. Author index at end of volume 2.

746. *Biblioteca de dialectología hispanoamericana*. Buenos Aires: Instituto de Filología, Universidad de Buenos Aires, 1930–49. 7 vols.

Contains a number of worthwhile bibliographies.

747. Ferguson, Charles A., and William A. Stewart. *Linguistic Reading Lists for Teachers of Modern Languages: French, German, Italian, Russian, Spanish*. Washington, D.C.: Center for Applied Linguistics, 1963. v + 114 pp.

Includes some journals dealing frequently with linguistics. Annotated bibliographic information. Virtually nothing transformational or structural.

748. Hall, Pauline C. *A Bibliography of Spanish Linguistics: Articles in Serial Publications*. Baltimore: Linguistic Society of America, 1957. 162 pp.

Contains author and word index. Published as a supplement to *Language* (vol. 32, no. 4 [October–December 1956]).

749. Lapointe, Jacques. *Bibliographie de l'espagnol d'Amérique*. Dakar: Centre de Hautes Etudes Afro-Ibero-Américaines de l'Université de Dakar, 1968. 105 pp.

Selective, unannotated bibliography of books and journal articles for all American countries where Spanish is spoken, including the United States.

750. Nichols, Madaline Wallis. *A Bibliographical Guide to Materials on American Spanish*. Cambridge, Mass.: Harvard University Press, 1941. 114 pp.

Annotated bibliography classified by country and subject. Still very useful. The following attempts have been made to supplement Nichols on a country-by-country or area-by-area basis: Hensley C. Woodbridge, "The Spanish of the American Southwest and Louisiana: A Bibliographical Survey for 1940–53," *Orbis* 3 (1954):236–44; Woodbridge, "Central American Spanish, A Bibliography (1940–53)," *Inter-American Review of Bibliography* 6 (1956):103–15; Woodbridge, "An Annotated Bibliography of Publications concerning the Spanish of Bolivia, Cuba, Ecuador, Paraguay, and Peru for the Years 1940–57," *Kentucky Foreign Language Quarterly* 7 (1960):37–54; Jack Emory Davis, "The Spanish of Argentina and Uruguay: An Annotated Bibliography for 1940–65," *Orbis* 15 (1966):160–89, 442–88; ibid. 17 (1968):232–77, 539–73; ibid. 19 (1970):205–32; ibid. 20 (1971):236–69; Davis, "The Spanish of Mexico: An Annotated Bibliography for 1940–69," *Hispania* 54 (1971):624–56; Michael Fody

III, "The Spanish of the American Southwest and Louisiana: A Bibliographical Survey for 1954–69," *Orbis* 19 (1970):529–40.

751. Quilis, Antonio. *Fonética y fonología del español.* Cuadernos Bibliográficos no. 10. Madrid: Consejo Superior de Investigaciones Científicas, 1963. 104 pp.

Useful basic bibliography which also contains a section on American Spanish.

752. Rice, Frank, and Allene Guss. *Information Sources in Linguistics.* Washington, D.C.: Center for Applied Linguistics, 1965. viii + 42 pp.

Attempts coverage of all major traditional fields of linguistics.

753. Rohlfs, Gerhard. *Manual de filología hispánica: Guía bibliográfica, crítica y metódica.* Translated by Carlos Patiño Rosselli. Bogota: Instituto Caro y Cuervo, 1957. 337 pp.

Studies dealing with language of the Iberian peninsula from prehistorical times. Includes Spanish America and Brazil.

754. Serís, Homero. *Bibliografía de la lingüística española.* Bogota: Instituto Caro y Cuervo, 1964. lix + 981 pp.

An extensive, fundamental bibliography that covers the following: general linguistics, Romance linguistics, Spanish linguistics, peninsular languages, Hispanic dialects (including Judeo-Spanish), American Spanish (including indigenous languages and the Spanish of the Philippines and Africa), and the teaching of Spanish. A number of the items are annotated, and many references to book reviews are given. Lengthy index and detailed table of contents.

755. Solé, Carlos A. *Bibliografía sobre el español en América, 1920–1967.* Washington, D.C.: Georgetown University Press, 1970. 175 pp.

Contains more than 1,450 items, many of which are annotated. Extremely detailed classified arrangement. Includes general and other linguistic studies and bibliographies as well as bibliographies and linguistic studies relating to all Spanish-speaking countries in America, including the United States.

756. Woodbridge, Hensley C., and Paul Olson. "A Tentative Bibliography of Hispanic Linguistics." Mimeographed. Urbana: University of Illinois, Department of Spanish, Portuguese, and Italian, 1952. xxii + 203 pp.

Classified selective bibliography based on works cited by Yakov Malkiel in his footnotes. The 1879 entries cover six main divisions: Vulgar and medieval Latin, comparative Romance linguistics, substrata, Catalan, Spanish, and Portuguese. Contains author index and word index.

General Works

757. Alonso, Amado. *Estudios lingüísticos: Temas españoles.* 3d ed. Madrid: Gredos, 1967 (1951). 286 pp.

A collection of essays that includes linguistic geography, phonemics, and stylistics.

758. ———. *Estudios lingüísticos: Temas hispanoamericanos.* 3d ed. Madrid: Gredos, 1967 (1953). 360 pp.

Includes such studies on the language of Spanish America as the linguistic basis of American Spanish and the origin of the *seseo*.

759. Cerdá Massó, Ramón. *Lingüística hoy.* Barcelona: Teide, 1969.

A clear, general introduction to contemporary linguistics.

760. Criado de Val, Manuel. *Fisonomía del idioma español: Sus características comparadas con las de francés, italiano, portugués, inglés y alemán.* 3d ed. Madrid: Aguilar, 1962 (1954). xv + 256 pp.

Concise work. Maps showing bilingual and dialectal zones. Also contains material on American Spanish.

761. *Current Trends in Linguistics.* Edited by Thomas A. Sebeok. Vol. 4, *Ibero-American and Caribbean Linguistics,* edited by Robert Lado, Norman A. McQuown, Sol Saporta, and Yolanda Lastra. The Hague: Mouton, 1968. 659 pp.

Part 1 deals with general and Ibero-American linguistics and has articles on phonology, lexicography, dialectology, and philology. Part 2 deals with the linguistics of non-Iberoamerican languages. Part 3 deals with such topics as bilingualism, language teaching in America, and applied linguistic research. Part 4 deals with the organization of linguistic activities and the present state of linguistics. This important work has articles by such well-known scholars as Yakov Malkiel, Juan M. Lope Blanch, and Robert A. Hall, Jr., in addition to the editors listed above.

762. Elcock, W. D. *The Romance Languages.* London: Faber & Faber; New York: Macmillan Co., 1960. 573 pp.

Good treatment of Spanish. Valuable for a broad view of the Romance linguistic world, it concentrates on the earlier stages of the languages.

763. *Enciclopedia lingüística hispánica.* Directed by M. Alvar et al. Madrid: Consejo Superior de Investigaciones Científicas, 1960–62.

Vol. 1 and supplements to vol. 1, 656 pp. Vol. 2 (1967), 460 pp. 6 vols. planned.

A scholarly treatment of the Spanish language. Chapters by specialists with bibliographic footnotes.

764. Posner, Rebecca. *The Romance Languages: A Linguistic Introduction.* Garden City, N.Y.: Doubleday & Co., 1966. 336 pp.

A comparative introduction to the major modern Romance languages (French, Italian, Spanish, Portuguese, and Rumanian). Analyzes the historical development, internal structure, and present-day variants and dialects of each language.

765. Vidos, B. E. *Manual de lingüística románica.* 2d ed. Madrid: Aguilar, 1973 (1963). xxiv + 416 pp. Translation of *Handbook tot de Romaanse Taalkunde* (1956).

A good general introduction. Covers such topics as the origin of Romance linguistics, Romance linguistics as a historical science, the comparative historical method, and twentieth-century Romance linguistics. Diagrams and bibliography.

Development of the Spanish Language

766. Baldinger, Kurt. *La formación de los dominios lingüísticos en la península ibérica.* Translated by Emilio Lledó and Monserrat Macau. 2d ed. Madrid: Gredos, 1969 (1958). 398 pp.

A thorough historical and comparative linguistic study. From Romanization through the Reconquest. Extensive bibliography and maps.

767. Bolaño e Isla, Amancio. *Manual de la historia de la lengua española.* 3d ed. Mexico: Porrúa, 1971 (1959). 221 pp.

A clear, well-organized introduction to the history of the Spanish language.

768. Entwistle, William J. *The Spanish Language.* Reprint. London: Faber & Faber, 1969 (1936). 367 pp. Spanish version, by Francisco Villar, *Las lenguas de España* (Madrid: Ediciones Istmo, 1972). 420 pp.

Traces the Spanish language from pre-Roman times to today. Spanish American included, as well as Portuguese, Catalan, and Basque.

769. Lapesa, Rafael. *Historia de la lengua española.* 7th ed. Madrid: Escelicer, 1968 (1942). 421 pp.

Standard work on language from pre-Roman times to the present.

Includes such topics as the Latin language in Spain, Arabic influence, archaic Spanish, modern Spanish, and Judeo-Spanish.
770. **Lenz, Rudolph.** *La oración y sus partes.* Madrid: Revista de Filología Española, 1920. 545 pp.
   Studies the Spanish language in its relation to linguistic psychology.
771. **Menéndez Pidal, Ramón.** *Orígenes del español: Estado lingüístico de la península ibérica hasta el siglo XI.* 5th ed. Madrid: Espasa-Calpe, 1964 (1926). xv + 592 pp. *El idioma español en sus primeros tiempos* (Madrid: Espasa-Calpe, 1964) is a synthesis of this work.
   The monumental work of Spanish historical linguistics covering the ninth through eleventh centuries.
772. **Oliver Asín, Jaíme.** *Historia de la lengua española.* 2d ed. Madrid: Diana Artes Gráficas, 1941 (1938). 254 pp.
   Introductory presentation intended for students. Divided into three parts: history of the language, phonetics, and morphology.
773. **Spaulding, Robert K.** *How Spanish Grew.* 2d ed. Berkeley and Los Angeles: University of California Press, 1968 (1943). 259 pp.
   A clearly presented, standard treatment of the development of the Spanish language.
774. **Trend, John B.** *The Language and History of Spain.* London: Hutchinson University Library, 1953. 189 pp.
   Brief discussion of the development of Spanish from medieval times to the present. Also includes Spanish-speaking America.

Dialectology

Only general works on Spanish and Spanish American dialectology are included in this section. Consult chapter 12 (pp. 107–10) for bibliographies of Hispanic dialectology, especially the books by Serís, Solé, Alvar, and Nichols, and the article by Avellaneda.
775. **Alvar, Manuel.** *Textos hispánicos dialectales: Antología histórica.* Madrid: Consejo Superior de Investigaciones Científicas, 1960. 2 vols. Supplement to *Revista de filología española,* vol. 73.
   Also contains texts from American Spanish in volume 2.
776. **García de Diego, Vicente.** *Manual de dialectología española.* 2d ed. Madrid: Instituto de Cultura Hispánica, 1959 (1946). 324 pp.
   A standard reference guide to the dialects of Spain and Spanish America. Also includes Judeo-Spanish.

777. **Lope Blanch, Juan M.** *El español de América*. Madrid: Alcalá, 1968. 150 pp.

This basic book for Spanish American dialectology contains general studies on all of Spanish America, methodology and geographic linguistics, substratum, and studies on individual nations.

778. **Pop, Sever.** *La dialectologie: Aperçu historique et méthodes d'enquêtes linguistiques*. Louvain: University of Louvain and UNESCO, 1950. 2 vols.

Deals with Romance dialectology in volume 1, and specifically with Spanish on pages 337–434. Extensive bibliography.

779. **Wagner, Max Leopold.** *Lingua e dialetti dell-America Spagnola*. Florence: Le Lingue Estere, 1949. 190 pp.

Offers a clear and substantial compendium of the main aspects of American Spanish, with particular reference to popular speech.

780. **Zamora Vicente, Alonso.** *Dialectología española*. 2d ed. Madrid: Gredos, 1967 (1960). 588 pp.

A basic reference work on dialects in Spain, with a final chapter on American Spanish. Contains a 31-page bibliographic guide.

Phonology and Phonetics

781. **Alarcos Llorach, Emilio.** *Fonología española*. 4th ed. Madrid: Gredos, 1965 (1954). 232 pp. Reprinted in 1968.

Contains examples, charts, and much bibliographic data. A good work, but probably not suited for the beginner. Prague school approach to the analysis of the phonological structure of Spanish.

782. **Alonso, Amado.** *De la pronunciación medieval a la moderna en español*. 2d ed. Madrid: Gredos, 1967–69 (1955). 2 vols.

Important series prepared for publication by Rafael Lapesa. A fundamental work that traces the history of Spanish pronunciation.

783. **Canfield, D. Lincoln.** *La pronunciación del español en América: Ensayo histórico-descriptivo*. Bogota: Instituto Caro y Cuervo, 1962. 103 pp.

Although rather limited in scope, it still is a significant attempt to characterize American Spanish. Accompanied by maps of linguistic peculiarities and has a lengthy bibliography.

784. **Cárdenas, Daniel.** *Introducción a una comparación fonológica del español y del inglés*. Washington, D.C.: Center for Applied Linguistics of the Modern Language Association of America, 1960. x + 63 pp.

Detailed contrastive treatment, including a great deal of supraseg-
mentals.
785. Dalbor, John V. *Spanish Pronunciation.* New York: Holt,
Rinehart & Winston, 1969. xi + 332 pp.

An introduction to phonetics and phonemics, an analysis of
Spanish phonology, and a manual of oral drill for English speakers.
Contains a lengthy bibliography.
786. Gili Gaya, Samuel. *Elementos de fonética general.* 5th ed.
Madrid: Gredos, 1966 (1950). 200 pp.

A basic introduction to Spanish phonetics. Bibliography.
787. Hadlich, Roger L., James S. Holton, and Matías Montes. *A
Drillbook of Spanish Pronunciation.* New York: Harper & Row,
1968. xviii + 236 pp. Tapes.

Brief explanations of problem areas in Spanish pronunciation for
speakers of English, followed by numerous exercises.
788. Harris, James W. *Spanish Phonology.* Cambridge, Mass.: MIT
Press, 1969. 218 pp.

An important contribution in that it represents an attempt to apply
Chomsky and Halle's *Sound Pattern of English* (New York: Harper
& Row, 1968), a transformational approach, to the description of
Spanish phonological universals.
789. Malmberg, Bertil. *Estudios de fonética hispánica.* Madrid: Con-
sejo Superior de Investigaciones Científicas, 1965. xv + 154 pp.

Ten of Malmberg's studies that also have related interest to American Spanish.
790. Navarro Tomás, Tomás. *Fonología española.* New York: Las
Americas, 1966 (1946). 217 pp. English translation, *Studies in
Spanish Phonology* (Coral Gables, Fla.: University of Miami Press,
1968). 160 pp.

Basic study on the development of Spanish phonology from the
Cid to Miró.
791. ———. *Manual de entonación española.* 2d ed. New York:
Hispanic Institute, 1948 (1944). 306 pp.

A basic study of Spanish entonation which also takes Spanish
American speech into account.
792. ———. *Manual de pronunciación español.* 17th ed. Madrid:
Revista de Filología Española, 1972 (1918). 328 pp.

A standard work on Spanish pronunciation. Only deals with
Castilian Spanish. Great wealth of articulatory phonetic data and
many sketches and diagrams.

793. Otero, Carlos-Peregrín. *Evolución y revolución en romance: Mínima introducción a la fonología.* Barcelona: Seix Barral, 1971. 318 pp.

Uses the contributions of Chomsky and J. W. Harris in his study of diachronic Romance phonology, with emphasis on *gallego-portugués* and Spanish. Extensive bibliography and useful indexes, maps, and an appendix which contains phonological processes.

794. Quilis, Antonio, and Joseph A. Fernández. *Curso de fonética y fonología españolas.* 7th ed., revised and enlarged. Madrid: Consejo Superior de Investigaciones Científicas, 1973 (1964). xxxii + 224 pp.

Sound, cogent treatment of theory and practice for English-speaking students. Contains many diagrams and sketches.

795. Saporta, Sol, and Heles Contreras. *A Phonological Grammar of Spanish.* Seattle: University of Washington Press, 1962. 43 pp.

Highly technical generative presentation of distinctive features of Spanish sounds.

796. Stockwell, Robert P., and J. Donald Bowen. *The Sounds of English and Spanish.* Chicago: University of Chicago Press, 1965. 168 pp.

Structural and contrastive approach to phonology incorporating audiolingual advances in language teaching.

Grammars, Morphology, and Syntax

797. Alarcos Llorach, Emilio. *Gramática estructural.* Reprint. Madrid: Gredos, 1969 (1951). 132 pp.

Structural grammar according to the School of Copenhagen, with special attention to the Spanish language.

798. Alonso, Amado, and Pedro Henríquez Ureña. *Gramática castellana.* 11th ed. Buenos Aires: Losada, 1953 (1939). 2 vols. Later editions.

Fundamental work. A thorough introduction to Spanish grammar with ample use of literary texts.

799. Bello, Andrés. *Gramática de lengua castellana.* 4th ed. Buenos Aires: Sopena, 1954 (1847). 541 pp. Notes by Rufino J. Cuervo in 2d pt.

Still a basic reference work for Spanish grammar.

800. Criado de Val, Manuel. *Síntesis de morfología española.* 2d ed.

Madrid: Consejo Superior de Investigaciones Científicas, 1961 (1952). 186 pp.

A fine introductory study intended primarily for non-native students of Spanish.

801. García de Diego, Vicente. *Gramática histórica española.* 3d ed. Madrid: Gredos, 1970 (1951). 624 pp.

History and origin of Spanish words with respect to phonetics, morphology, and syntax.

802. Gili Gaya, Samuel. *Curso superior de sintaxis española.* 8th ed. Barcelona: Spes, 1961 (1943). 347 pp.

A well-organized and clear exposition of Spanish syntax intended for students.

803. ⸺. *Nociones de gramática histórica española.* 2d ed. Barcelona: Spes, 1962 (1952). 102 pp.

Concise and clear presentation of the development of the Spanish language designed for students.

804. Hadlich, Roger L. *A Transformational Grammar of Spanish.* Englewood Cliffs, N.J.: Prentice-Hall, 1971. Spanish version, *Gramática transformativa del español* (Madrid: Gredos, 1973). 464 pp.

The only attempt at a complete transformational grammar of Spanish, based largely on Chomsky's *Aspects of the Theory of Syntax.*

805. Kany, Charles E. *American-Spanish Syntax.* 2d ed. Chicago: University of Chicago Press, 1951 (1945). xiii + 467 pp. Spanish version, *Sintaxis hispanoamericana* (Madrid: Gredos, 1969). 550 pp.

Treats the most important tendencies of American-Spanish syntax, with emphasis on popular expression.

806. Lorenzo, Emilio. *El español de hoy, lengua en ebullición.* Madrid: Gredos, 1966. 177 pp.

Eight studies on morphology, syntax, and phonology of present-day Spanish, with emphasis on the verb.

807. Menéndez Pidal, Ramón. *Manual de gramática histórica española.* 13th ed. Madrid: Espasa-Calpe, 1966 (1904). vii + 367 pp.

A fundamental work.

808. Ramsey, Marathon M., and Robert K. Spaulding. *A Textbook of Modern Spanish.* 2d ed. New York: Holt, Rinehart & Winston, 1956 (1894). xix + 692 + xvii pp.

A classic work revised by Spaulding. Valuable reference.

809. Real Academia Española. *Esbozo de una nueva gramática de la lengua española.* Madrid: Espasa-Calpe, 1973 (1931). 592 pp.

A standard reference which comprehensively covers Spanish grammar. This edition has a totally new section on phonology, a revised section on morphology, and an updated section on syntax. American as well as peninsular Spanish is covered.

810. Spaulding, Robert K. *Syntax of the Spanish Verb.* 2d ed. Liverpool: University Press, 1967 (1952). xx + 136 pp.

Concise explanation of the principal uses of the Spanish verb as found in modern writings.

811. Stevenson, C. H. *The Spanish Language Today.* London: Hutchinson University Library, 1970. 146 pp.

Concise survey of the Spanish language, and not a study of grammar. Deals with the phonetic system, verbs, definite and indefinite articles, word order, word formation, and other topics. Basic bibliography included.

812. Stockwell, Robert P., J. D. Bowen, and J. W. Martin. *Grammatical Structures of English and Spanish.* Chicago: University of Chicago Press, 1965. xi + 328 pp.

A contrastive approach to morphology and syntax with much information on methodology of teaching Spanish.

Dictionaries

Bibliographies

813. *Bibliographie der Wörterbucher/Bibliography of Dictionaries, 1945–1961.* Warsaw: Wydawnictwa Naukowo-Techniczne, 1965. xxxii + 248 pp.

814. Bibliography of Interlingual Scientific and Technical Dictionaries. 5th ed. Paris: UNESCO, 1969 (1951). 320 pp.

Lists several thousand dictionaries by language and subject. Many general dictionaries are also included.

815. Collison, Robert L. *Dictionaries of Foreign Languages: A Bibliographic Guide to General and Technical Dictionaries of the Chief Foreign Languages, with Historical and Explanatory Notes and Reference.* 2d ed. New York: Hafner Publishing Co., 1971 (1955). 303 pp.

Also contains useful bibliography.

816. Marton, T. W. *Foreign Language and English Dictionaries in the Physical Sciences and Engineering.* U.S. National Bureau of

Standards. Washington, D.C.: Government Printing Office, 1964. 189 pp.

Covers more than 2,800 items published from 1951 to 1962. Most items are English-based.

817. Saur, K. O. *Technik und Wirtschaft in fremden Sprachen: Internationale Bibliographie der Fachwörterbuch.* 3d ed. Munich: Verlag Dokumentation, 1966. cxlvi + 304 pp.

Fullest list of current language dictionaries; contains 3,632 items in 12 sections. Supplement (1967) has 967 entries. No annotations.

818. Walford, A. J., ed. *A Guide to Foreign Language Grammars and Dictionaries.* 2d ed. London: Library Association, 1967 (1964). 240 pp.

Annotated entries—complete bibliography, critical analyses, and contents. Pages 67–88 devoted to Spanish.

819. Zaunmüller, Wolfram. *Bibliographisches Handbuch der Sprachwörterbucher; ein Internationales Verzeichnis von 5600 Wörterbuchern der Jahre 1460–1958 für mehr als 500 Sprachen und Dialekte.* Stuttgart: A. Hiersemann, 1958. 496 columns.

A number of Spanish dictionaries are included.

General (including historical, etymological, and grammatical)

820. Alemany y Bolufer, José. *Nuevo diccionario de la lengua española.* Barcelona: Sopena, 1964 (1957). 1,130 pp.

Gives both peninsular and American usages.

821. Alonso Pedraz, Martín. *Enciclopedia del idioma: Diccionario histórico y moderno de la lengua española (siglos XII al XX) etimológico, tecnológico, regional e hispanoamericano.* Madrid: Aguilar, 1958. 3 vols.

Explains meaning and evolution of 30,000 Spanish and Spanish American words based on the authority of more than 1,500 authors from the Middle Ages to the present.

822. Boggs, R. S., L. Kasten, H. Keniston, and H. B. Richardson. "Tentative Dictionary of Medieval Spanish." Mimeographed. Chapel Hill: University of North Carolina Press, 1946. 2 vols.

Useful list, in process of being expanded.

823. Cejador y Frauca, Julio. *Vocabulario medieval castellano.* Reprint. New York: Las Americas, 1968 (1929). xii + 414 pp.

Alphabetical listing of words no longer used or those with different meanings. Examples given from medieval texts.

824. Corominas, Juan. *Breve diccionario etimológico de la lengua castellana.* 3d ed. Madrid: Gredos, 1973 (1961). 628 pp.

Abbreviated, revised edition of Corominas's four-volume work (see next entry).

825. ———. *Diccionario crítico etimológico de la lengua castellana.* 2d ed. Bern: A. Francke AG., 1970 (1954–57). 4 vols.

Each entry begins with generally accepted etymology and then offers more speculative etymology. Gives passages to demonstrate use of word in written works, bibliographic data, and complete lexicographical data.

826. Covarrubias, Sebastián de. *Tesoro de la lengua castellana o española.* Edited by M. de Riquer. Barcelona: S. A. Horta, 1943 (1611). 1,093 pp.

Famous dictionary of the seventeenth century. This edition is based on the original, with additions of Benito Remigio Noydens (1647).

827. *Duden español: Diccionario por la imagen.* London: Harrap, 1963. 672 + 111 + 128 pp.

One of the well-known Duden dictionaries. First part consists of illustrations grouped by subjects. On page opposite each illustration are listed the Spanish terms.

828. Fontecha, Carlos. *Glosario de voces comentadas en ediciones de textos clásicos.* Madrid: Consejo Superior de Investigaciones Científicas, 1941. viii + 409 pp.

Compilation of definitions taken from numerous critical editions. Of great value for reading literature of past centuries.

829. Gili Gaya, Samuel. *Tesoro lexicográfico (1492–1726).* Madrid: Consejo Superior de Investigaciones Científicas, 1947–57. 4 fascicles (A–E).

This valuable contribution is a compilation of lexicographical works from Nebrija's grammar to the first dictionary of the Royal Academy.

830. Martínez Amador, Emilio. *Diccionario gramatical.* Barcelona: Sopena, 1961. 1,498 pp.

Explanations of grammatical and rhetorical terms, orthography, and abbreviations.

831. Moliner, María. *Diccionario de uso del español.* Madrid: Gredos, 1966–67. 2 vols.

Serves as a dictionary of synonyms, and of accepted grammatical usage. Resolves doubts about expressions and constructions.

832. Oelschlager, Victor R. B. "A Medieval Spanish Word List." Mimeographed. Madison: University of Wisconsin Press, 1940. x + 230 pp.

Very useful list, based on published texts from the tenth century to Berceo. Author attempts to date first appearance of words.

833. *Pequeño Larousse ilustrado.* 14th ed. Buenos Aires: Larousse, 1964 (1912). viii + 1,663 pp. Later editions.

Good dictionary plus an encyclopedia section (history, geography, and biography) of almost 600 pages. Many illustrations.

834. Real Academia Española. *Diccionario de la lengua castellana.* Facsimile ed. Madrid: Gredos, 1963. 3 vols. (1726–39, 6 vols.).

This masterpiece, usually called *Diccionario de autoridades,* was the Spanish Royal Academy's first dictionary and is still a rich source for contemporary researchers.

835. ———. *Diccionario de la lengua española.* 19th ed. Madrid: Real Academia Española/Espasa-Calpe, 1970 (1726–39). xxix + 1,424 pp.

The standard authority on current usage published by the Spanish Royal Academy.

836. ———. *Diccionario histórico de la lengua española.* Madrid: Real Academia Española, 1960–. 8 fascicles (1970).

Compilation of the different usages of each word through the centuries.

837. ———. *Diccionario manual e ilustrado de la lengua española.* 2d ed. Madrid: Espasa-Calpe, 1950. xi + 1,572 pp.

Based on the sixteenth and seventeenth editions of the *Diccionario de la Academia,* and at the same time a supplement because it lists new words, including Spanish American words, which have not received the official approval of the academy.

838. Seco, Manuel. *Diccionario de dudas y dificultades de la lengua española.* 5th ed. Madrid: Aguilar, 1967 (1956). xx + 516 pp.

Aid in solving grammatical and lexical difficulties. Bibliography. Information on orthography and prosody.

839. *Vox: Diccionario general ilustrado de la lengua española.* Prologue by R. Menéndez Pidal. Revised by S. Gili Gaya. Barcelona: Spes, 1961 (1945). xxxix + 1,814 pp.

Authoritative, comprehensive, up to date. Gives etymology and synonyms and includes Central and South American words.

American Spanish

840. Kany, Charles E. *American-Spanish Euphemisms.* Berkeley and Los Angeles: University of California Press, 1960. xiii + 249 pp.

An important contribution, together with its companion volume (see next entry) to lexicology and semantics in Spanish America.

841. ———. *American-Spanish Semantics.* Berkeley and Los Angeles: University of California Press, 1960. viii + 352 pp. Spanish translation, *Semántica hispanoamericana* (Madrid: Aguilar, 1962).

First comprehensive volume on the subject. Special emphasis on popular speech. Explains how American Spanish differs from the Spanish norm. Bibliography of about 300 titles and 27-page word index.

842. Malaret, Augusto. *Diccionario de americanismos (con un índice científico de fauna y flora).* 3d ed. Buenos Aires: Emecé, 1946 (1925). 835 pp.

Lists Spanish words which have different meanings in America. Considered by some to be the most important and complete work on the Spanish of America.

843. Morínigo, Marcos A. *Diccionario manual de americanismos.* Buenos Aires: Muchnik, 1966. 738 pp.

Includes words, phrases, idioms, Indian terms, Latin American etymologies, and the like. Contains a 46-page bibliography of great value for books and articles dealing with regionalisms.

844. Santamaría, Francisco J. *Diccionario general de americanismos.* Mexico: Pedro Robredo, 1942–43. 3 vols.

Includes common and scientific equivalents for flora and fauna. Useful tool for Mexicanisms.

Bilingual

845. *Collins Spanish-English English-Spanish Dictionary.* Compiled by Colin Smith, in collaboration with M. Bermejo Marcos and E. Chang-Rodríguez. London: Collins, 1971. xxxviii + 1,242 pp.

A well-organized, up-to-date dictionary which embraces British and American English and peninsular and South American Spanish. According to some lexicographers, this is the best dictionary of its type.

846. Cuyás, Arturo, L. E. Brett, and H. S. Eaton. *Appleton's*

Revised English-Spanish and Spanish-English Dictionary. New York: Appleton-Century-Crofts, 1961 (1903). xxxii + 697 pp.

A good dictionary which has been used by several generations of students.

847. Gerrard, A. Bryson, and José de Heras Heras. *Cassell's Beyond the Dictionary in Spanish: A Handbook of Everyday Usage.* 2d ed., revised and enlarged. New York: Funk & Wagnalls, 1973 (1953). 226 pp.

Gives British and American translations. Usage of terms relating to household, office, automobile, food, and so forth. Attempts to bridge gap between Spanish acquired from grammar books and that spoken by natives.

848. Gillhoff, Gerd A., and P. Morales. *Crowell's Spanish-English and English-Spanish Dictionary.* New York: Thomas Y. Crowell Co., 1963. xii + 1,261 pp.

Many Spanish American expressions. Special attention to commercial Spanish. Designed for student, businessman, and tourist. Not as complete as many other dictionaries.

849. *Gran diccionario general: Inglés-español español-inglés.* Madrid: EDAF, 1966. 2 vols.

Contains archaic words useful for reading classical texts, neologisms for Spain and Spanish America, and many colloquial expressions.

850. Peers, E. A., et al., eds. *Cassell's Spanish Dictionary: Spanish-English English-Spanish.* New York: Funk & Wagnalls, 1960 (1959). xvi + 1,477 pp.

A good dictionary that reflects British English.

851. Raventós, Margaret. *McKay's Modern Spanish-English English-Spanish Dictionary.* New York: David McKay, 1962 (1953). xii + 1,230 pp.

Brief entries. This dictionary, suitable mainly for undergraduate students, is very careful in distinguishing different meanings. Oriented toward England and Spain.

852. *Simon and Schuster's International Dictionary: English/Spanish Spanish/English.* New York: Simon & Schuster, 1973. xviii + 1,605 pp.

More than 200,000 entries, including Latin American, Iberian, American, and British variants; regionalisms; and technical and scientific terminology.

853. Smith, C. C., G. A. Davies, and H. B. Hall. *Langenscheidt's Standard Dictionary of the English and Spanish Languages.* New York: Barnes & Noble, 1966. 1,071 pp.

Words and expressions are British and Castilian. A good smaller dictionary.

854. Velázquez de la Cadena, Mariano, E. Gray, and J. L. Iribas. *A New Pronouncing Dictionary of the Spanish and English Languages.* Chicago: Follett Publishing Co., 1967 (1852). 1,488 pp.

An old standby that has been somewhat modernized in recent editions.

855. Williams, Edwin B. *Spanish and English Dictionary/Diccionario inglés y español.* New York: Holt, Rinehart & Winston, 1962 (1957). 1,226 pp. Expanded version published in 1963 (1,243 pp.)

Good, well-organized dictionary that marked an advance over those of this type published previously.

Familiar Quotations, Proverbs, and Idioms

856. Caballero, Ramón. *Diccionario de modismos de la lengua castellana.* 1st Argentine ed. Buenos Aires: Librería El Ateneo, 1942 (1905). 1,179 pp.

More than 60,000 idioms, with clear explanations in Spanish.

857. Correas, Gonzalo. *Vocabulario de refranes y frases proverbiales y otras fórmulas comunes de la lengua castellana.* Madrid: Real Academia Española, 1906 (based on a manuscript of 1627–30). 633 pp. Rev. ed., Bordeaux: Institut d'Etudes Ibériques et Ibero-Américaines de l'Université de Bordeaux, 1967.

Abundant collection of phrases current in Correas's time.

858. Goicoechea Romano, Cesáreo. *Diccionario de citas verdades y semiverdades, axiomas y paradojas, flores del genio y del ingenio de los grandes pensadores, escritores y hombres célebres de todos los tiempos, compilados en más de 12.500 frases y ordenados según sus materias.* 2d ed. Madrid: Labor, 1962 (1952). 880 pp.

Indexed by abstract idea (*ángeles, burlas, fantasía,* etc.) and also contains alphabetical indexes of authors and phrases.

859. Harbettle, Thomas B., and Martin Hume. *Dictionary of Quotations (Spanish).* New York: Frederick Ungar, 1958. 462 pp.

Explanations of quotations; also translations into English. Subject and author indexes.

860. Martínez Kleiser, Luis. *Refranero general ideológico español.* Madrid: Real Academia Española, 1953. xix + 783 pp.

An extensive compilation of familiar sayings.

861. Recio Flores, Sergio. *Diccionario comparado de refranes y modismos: Spanish-English.* Mexico: Libros de México, 1968. xv + 391 pp.

Many useful expressions in Spanish and English listings. Contains bibliography of many types of lexical works.

862. Sintes Pros, Jorge. *Diccionario de aforismos, proverbios y refranes: Con su interpretación para el empleo adecuado y con equivalencias en cinco idiomas.* 4th ed. Barcelona: Sintes, 1967 (1961). 894 pp.

Explained in French, Italian, English, German, and Latin. Section on Latin proverbs, expressions, and legal terminology.

863. ———. *Diccionario de máximas, pensamientos y sentencias.* 6th rev. ed. Barcelona: Sintes, 1964. 591 pp.

A useful, popular work.

864. ———. *Gran diccionario de frases célebres.* Barcelona: Sintes, 1961. 3 vols.

Contains 40,000 Spanish and foreign quotes on history, philosophy, and literature.

865. Vega, Vicente. *Diccionario ilustrado de frases célebres y citas literarias.* 3d ed. Barcelona: Gustavo Gili, 1962 (1952). 939 pp.

Spanish and foreign quotations.

Synonyms and Antonyms

866. Andrés, M. F. *Diccionario español de sinónimos y equivalencias.* 5th ed. Barcelona: Aedos, 1969. 383 pp.

867. Barcia, Roque. *Diccionario de sinónimos castellanos.* 3d ed. Buenos Aires: Librería el Ateneo, 1944 (1939). 735 pp.

Also contains an extensive analytical index of the expressions and meanings cited or explained in the synonyms included in the work.

868. Casares y Sánchez, Julio. *Diccionario ideológico de la lengua española desde la idea a la palabra, desde la palabra a la idea.* Barcelona: Gustavo Gili, 1966 (1942). 1,446 pp.

Divided into three parts: synoptic, analogic, and the dictionary proper. The first two parts are set out like Roget's *Thesaurus*.

869. *Diccionario de sinónimos, antónimos e ideas afines.* Buenos Aires: Editorial Andina, 1970. 213 pp.

A handy list in three columns: *palabras, sinónimos, antónimos.*

870. *Diccionario de sinónimos e ideas afines y de la rima.* Madrid: Paraninfo, Joaquim Horta Massanes (Barcelona), 1970. 363 pp.
An alphabetical listing like Roget's *Thesaurus.*

871. *Diccionario de sinónimos, ideas afines y contrarios.* London: Harrap, 1967. 536 pp.

872. Gili Gaya, S. *Diccionario de sinónimos.* Barcelona: Vox, 1958. xvi + 844 pp.
Interesting introduction and a well-organized and well-presented work.

873. Sáinz de Robles, Federico C. *Diccionario español de sinónimos y antónimos.* Madrid: Aguilar, 1963. 1,150 pp.
Format of Roget's *Thesaurus.*

Linguistic Terminology

874. Lázaro Carreter, Fernando. *Diccionario de términos filológicos.* 3d ed. Madrid: Gredos, 1968 (1953). 444 pp.
Concise definitions with equivalents in foreign languages. At the end of the work there is a list of German, English, and French terms with Spanish equivalents.

875. Pei, Mario A. *Glossary of Linguistic Terminology.* New York: Doubleday & Co., 1966. 299 pp.
Most common linguistic terminology. Where authorities differ in their uses of a term, Pei gives several definitions, attributing each to the particular linguist.

876. Steible, Daniel J. *Concise Handbook of Linguistics: A Glossary of Terms.* New York: Philosophical Library, 1967. 146 pp.
Although intended for the student of English linguistics, this alphabetical listing can be useful for American students in other languages. Offers brief and simplified explanations.

877. Walsh, Donald D. *"What's What": A List of Useful Terms for Teachers of Modern Languages.* New York: MLA, 1963. 31 pp.
Defines a number of terms from the field of linguistics. Included in *A Handbook for Teachers of Spanish and Portuguese,* edited by D. D. Walsh (Boston: D. C. Heath & Co., 1969), pp. 303–25.

Slang

The two best slang dictionaries are listed below. For bibliographies which list slang dictionaries for the Hispanic world, consult Serís (no. 754) and Solé (no. 755).

878. Besses, Luis. *Diccionario de argot español o lenguaje jergal, gitano, delincuente profesional y popular.* Barcelona: Sucesores de Manuel Soler, 1905. 277 pp. Many later editions.
Divided into two parts: slang-standard vocabulary and standard vocabulary-slang. Still a standard dictionary of peninsular Spanish slang.

879. Trejo, Arnulfo D. *Diccionario etimológico latinoamericano del léxico de la delincuencia.* Mexico: UTEHA, 1968. 226 pp.
Mostly represents the jargon of the delinquents of Mexico City, but also includes the slang words spoken in Lima, Argentina, Brazil, Chile, Colombia, Panama, and southwestern United States. Trejo provides simple definitions and, wherever possible, the origins of the slang words. He has utilized the lexical studies of many Latin American and Spanish scholars and some Hispanic literary works for his definitions and etymologies. The largest sections cover thievery, fighting, and the authorities delinquents encounter, but also includes sections on penal institutions, parts of the body, dress, money, and the like. Extensive bibliography and index of words studied.

13 Scholarly Periodicals

Bibliographies and Guides to Periodicals

880. Bleznick, Donald W. "A Guide to Journals in the Hispanic Field: A Selected Annotated List of Journals Central to the Study of Spanish and Spanish American Language and Literature." *Hispania* 49 (October 1966):569–83 and 52 (October 1969):723–37; rev. ed., 55 (March 1972):207–21.

Fully annotated and indexed list of some 80 scholarly journals, both current and defunct. Provides information on types of articles, book reviews, and bibliographies. Other useful information.

881. Carter, Boyd G. *Historia de la literatura hispanoamericana a través de sus revistas.* Mexico: Ediciones de Andrea, 1968. 271 pp.

Studies a large number of Spanish American literary publications from before Independence up to the 1960s. Extensive bibliography.

882. ————. *Las revistas literarias de Hispanoamérica: Breve historia y contenido.* Mexico: Ediciones de Andrea, 1959. 282 pp.

Information on important literary journals and on development of periodical literature and literary and philosophical currents.

883. *Catálogo de las publicaciones periódicas madrileñas existentes en la Hemeroteca Municipal de Madrid, 1661–1930.* Madrid: Artes Gráficas Municipales, 1933–.

More than 3,000 titles for the years 1661–1930, listed chronologically and alphabetically. Information on frequency of publication, size, number of pages, and dates.

884. Charno, Steven M., comp. *Latin American Newspapers in United States Libraries: A Union List.* Austin: University of Texas Press, 1969. 619 pp.

Detailed data on holdings of 70 libraries, with approximately 5,500 titles. Arrangement based on place of publication, first by country, then by city. Twenty Latin American republics and Puerto Rico represented.

885. Forster, Merlin H. *An Index to Mexican Literary Periodicals.* New York: Scarecrow Press, 1966. iii + 276 pp.

Index to 16 periodicals which began between 1920 and 1960.

886. Grossman, Jorge, ed. *Index to Latin American Periodicals: Humanities and Social Sciences.* Boston: G. K. Hall & Co., 1961–. Has author and title indexes. Supplements the eight-volume *Index to Latin American Periodical Literature, 1929–1960* (see no. 91). Since volume 3 (1965), it has been published by Scarecrow Press, Metuchen, N.J.

887. Guerrero, Fuensanta, Antonio Quilis, and Juan Manuel Rozas. *La lengua y la literatura en el Consejo Superior de Investigaciones Científicas.* Madrid: Consejo Superior de Investigaciones Científicas, 1965. 324 pp.

Contains 3,000 titles on language and literature mainly taken from the books and journals of the Instituto Miguel de Cervantes of the CSIC. The years covered are chiefly 1940–64, but also included are issues of the *Revista de filología española* and its *anejos* for the years 1914–37. Also indexes the *Boletín de filología española, Revista de literatura, Cuadernos de literatura, Cuadernos de literatura contemporánea, Anales cervantinos, Revista de bibliografía nacional,* and *Revista bibliográfica y documental.*

888. "Indice general de publicaciones periódicas cubanas." Mimeographed. Humanidades y ciencias sociales, no. 1. Havana: Biblioteca Nacional José Martí, 1970. 191 pp.

A systematic attempt to compile an index to periodical articles in 48 Cuban journals.

889. Lafleur, Héctor René, Sergio D. Provenzano, and Fernando P. Alonso. *Las revistas argentinas, 1893–1967.* Rev. ed. Buenos Aires: Centro Editor de América Latina, 1969. 351 pp.

A panorama of Argentine literary journals is given in chronological order with emphasis on literary groups and movements. An index of journals concludes the study.

890. Leavitt, Sturgis E., et al., eds. *Revistas hispanoamericanas: Indice bibliográfico, 1843–1935.* Santiago de Chile: Fondo Histórico y Bibliográfico José Toribio Medina, 1960. xxii + 589 pp.

A listing and description of the most representative magazines. Items are grouped according to subject.

891. Levi, Nadia, et al., eds. *Guía de publicaciones periódicas de universidades latinoamericanas.* Mexico: Universidad Nacional Autónoma de México, 1967. 406 pp.

Divided by country. Each national section contains alphabetical listing with bibliographic information.

New Serial Titles. See no. 26.

892. **Pan American Union.** *Index to Latin American Periodical Literature, 1929–1960.* Boston: G. K. Hall & Co., 1962. 8 vols. 1961–65 Supplement published in 1968. (See also no. 886.)

Besides Latin American journals, some from elsewhere are included if subject or author is Latin American. Covers all cultural aspects.

893. **Shelby, Charmion, ed.** *Latin American Periodicals Currently Received in the Library of Congress and in the Library of the Department of Agriculture.* Washington, D.C.: Library of Congress, 1944. vii + 249 pp.

Basic information about serial literature except newspapers.

894. **Titus, Edna Brown.** *Union List of Serials in the Libraries of the United States and Canada.* 3d ed. New York: H. W. Wilson & Co., 1965. 5 vols.

Each entry includes bibliographic data. Holdings of more than 600 libraries are included.

895. **Tortajada, Amadeo, and C. de Amaniel.** *Materiales de investigación: Indice de artículos de revistas del Consejo Superior de Investigaciones Científicas, 1939–1949.* Madrid: Consejo Superior de Investigaciones Científicas, 1952. 2 vols.

Author-subject index to 128 reviews of the CSIC for the years indicated.

Ulrich's International Periodicals Directory. See no. 31.

896. *Union List of Periodicals in the Romance Languages and Literatures in the British National, University, and Special Libraries.* London: University of London Library, 1964. vi + 150 pp.

Several hundred periodicals are listed.

897. **Zimmerman, Irene.** *A Guide to Current Latin American Periodicals: Humanities and Social Sciences.* Gainesville, Fla.: Kallman, 1961. 357 pp.

Extensive coverage and very informative annotated listing by country. Chapter 4 has a chronological listing. Contains an annotated bibliography of reference sources.

898. **Zubatsky, David S.** "A Bibliography of Cumulative Indexes to Hispanic American Language and Literary Reviews of the Nineteenth and Twentieth Centuries." *Revista Interamericana de Bibliografía* 20, no. 1 (January–March 1970):28–57.

Annotated bibliography of some 180 journals published in Latin America and the United States.

899. ———. "A Bibliography of Cumulative Indexes to Spanish Lan-

guage and Literary Reviews of the Nineteenth and Twentieth Centuries.'' *Hispania* 51 (October 1968):622–28.

Aims to include all periodicals dealing with the Spanish and Catalan languages and literatures published in Spain during the periods covered.

Major Journals in
the Hispanic Field

The following annotated list of journals central to the study of Spanish and Spanish American literatures and languages includes current and defunct scholarly periodicals taken from the original version of my ''Guide to Journals in the Hispanic Field'' (*Hispania* 49 [1966]:469–83 and 52 [1969]:723–37) and the revised edition (*Hispania* 55 [1972]:207–21), and several new journals are listed. The expanded list now comprises 100 important twentieth-century journals. It should be emphasized that, as in previous versions, this is a selected list of journals which have a substantial frequency of articles, bibliography, book reviews, and additional material related to the study of Hispanic language and literature. The choice of journals, based on my experience and the suggestions of colleagues, aims to provide a basic compilation of periodical publications from throughout the Hispanic world, the United States, and several European countries.

The items included in each annotation, when available and applicable, are found in the following order: title; subtitle; *PMLA* or other standard abbreviation (if title is longer than one word); original place of publication; date the journal began, and if defunct, the date it ceased publication; frequency; publishing organization and address; director or editor; index(es) of its contents; supplements it has published; language(s) of the text; nature of the articles and book reviews; and other pertinent information. CSIC is the abbreviation for the Consejo Superior de Investigaciones Científicas.

A number of the journals below are indexed in Guerrero's and Tortajada's compilations (nos. 887 and 895, respectively, of this *Sourcebook*).

900. *Abside: Revista de cultura mejicana.* Mexico, 1937–. Quarterly. Published at Plateros 76, Mexico 19, D.F., Mexico. Directed by Alfonso Junco. Indexes: 1937–56 in vol. 20 (1956); 1957–61 in vol. 25 (1961); 1962–66 in vol. 30 (1966).

Text in Spanish. Articles on literature and philosophy. Excerpts from Mexican writers; original poetry and short stories mainly by Mexican authors.

901. *Al-Andalus: Revista de las Escuelas de Estudios Arabes de Madrid y Granada* (*Andalus*). Madrid, 1933–. Semiannual. Published by the CSIC, Patronato Menéndez y Pelayo, Instituto Miguel Asín, Medinaceli 4, Madrid 14, Spain. Directed by Emilio García Gómez. *Indice de los veinte primeros volúmenes* (Madrid: CSIC, 1962), 286 pp., indexed in Tortajada.

Text in French, Spanish, and English. Articles and book reviews on Hispanic and Arabic studies in linguistics, literature, history, art, and philosophy. Includes lists of doctoral dissertations and necrology.

902. *Anales cervantinos* (*A Cerv*). Madrid, 1951–. Annual. Published by the CSIC, Instituto Miguel de Cervantes de Filología Hispánica, Duque de Medinaceli 4, Madrid 14, Spain. Directed by Francisco Maldonado de Guevara. Annual index.

Text in Spanish. Articles on Cervantes, the *Quijote,* and themes applicable to Cervantes and other authors of his period. Includes a section entitled ''Crónica cervantina,'' on people, books, studies, and other matter related to Cervantes. Contains reviews of books dealing with Cervantes or any of his works, and a ''Bibliografía cervantina.''

903. *Anales de la Universidad de Chile* (*AUC*). Santiago, 1843–. Quarterly. Published by the Universidad de Chile, Casilla 10-D, Santiago, Chile. Directed by Alvaro Bunster. *Indice general, 1843–1950* (Santiago: Editorial Universitaria, 1954), 285 pp.

Text in Spanish. Articles and book reviews on literature deal mostly with Spanish America. Publishes *homenaje* issues.

904. *Anales galdosianos* (*An G*). Pittsburgh, Pa., 1966–. Annual. Published at the University of Texas, Austin, Texas 78712. Directed by Rodolfo Cardona.

Text in Spanish and English. Articles, texts, and documents on Galdós's work and period and on theoretical problems of the realistic novel. Descriptive classified bibliography for 1966–67 (in 1968) covering publications of and about Galdós. Each issue contains a bibliography of the preceding year.

905. *Anuario de letras: Revista de la Facultad de Filosofía y Letras.* Mexico, 1961–. Annual. Published by the Facultad de Filosofía y Letras, Universidad Nacional Autónoma de México, Ciudad Universitaria, Mexico 20, D.F., Mexico. Edited by Juan M. Lope Blanch.

Text in Spanish. Articles, notes, and book reviews on Mexican and other Hispanic literatures and languages.

906. *Anuario martiano.* Havana, 1969–. Annual. Published by the Sala Martí, Biblioteca Nacional de Cuba, Havana, Cuba. Text in Spanish. Articles devoted to all phases of the life and work of José Martí. Includes book reviews, notes, and an extensive bibliography.

907. *Arbor: Revista general de investigación y cultura.* Madrid, 1944–. Monthly. Published by the CSIC, Duque de Medinaceli 4, Madrid 14, Spain. Directed by Pedro Rocamora Valls. Annual index and *Indices de los setenta y cinco primeros números* (Madrid: CSIC, 1952), 1,600 pp., in Tortajada.
Articles and book reviews on culture and literature.

908. *Archivo de filología aragonesa (AFA).* Zaragoza, 1945–. Annual. Published by CSIC, Institución Fernando el Católico, Palacio de la Diputación Provincial, Zaragoza, Spain. Directed by Manuel Alvar. Indexed in Tortajada.
Text in Spanish and French. Articles and book reviews on linguistics of Spain and Portugal, and Spanish dialects, especially *aragonés*. Many lists of various lexicological distinctions found in certain areas of Spain.

909. *Archivum* (Oviedo) *(AO).* Oviedo, 1951–. 3 issues per year. Published by the Facultad de Filosofía y Letras, Universidad de Oviedo, Spain. Directed by E. Alarcos Llorach and J. Ma. Martínez Cachero.
Text in Spanish. Articles and book reviews on linguistics and some on peninsular Spanish literature.

910. *Archivum linguisticum: A Review of Comparative Philology and General Linguistics (ArL).* Glasgow, 1949–. Semiannual. Published by the University of Glasgow. Edited by I. M. Campbell and T. F. Mitchell.
Text mainly in English and French but also in German, Italian, and Spanish. Articles frequently on Spanish topics. Book reviews and list of books received.

911. *Asomante: Revista literaria.* San Juan, 1945–70; 1972–. Quarterly. Published by the Asociación de Graduadas de la Universidad de Puerto Rico, Apartado Postal 1142, San Juan, Puerto Rico 00902. Directed by Venus Lidia Soto. *Indices de "Asomante" (1945–1959)* (San Juan: Instituto de Cultura Puertorriqueña, 1963), 82 pp.
Text in Spanish. Articles and book reviews mainly on Hispanic

literature. Also includes original poetry, short stories, and correspondence from Spain, Italy, and Paris on current literary affairs.

912. *Atenea: Revista trimestral de ciencias, letras y artes.* Concepción, 1924–. Title changed to *Nueva atenea* for nos. 423–24 (1970) and back to *Atenea* with no. 425 (1972). Published by the Universidad de Concepción, Chile. Directed by Milton Rossel. *Indice general* for 1924–50, compiled by Arthur E. Gropp (Washington, D.C.: Pan American Union, 1955), 205 pp.

Text in Spanish. Articles on Hispanic literature and long book reviews on Hispanic and general literature. Also concerned with culture and art. Some numbers are *homenajes;* for example, two issues (1967) are devoted to Darío.

913. *Boletín de dialectología española (BDE).* Barcelona, 1941–68. Continued the *Butlletí de dialectología catalana* (1913–36). Annual. Published by the Instituto Internacional de Cultura Románica . . . de Barcelona. Directed by A. Griera.

Text in Spanish, French, and Catalan. Articles mostly on Spanish linguistics and dialectology. Most of each issue is devoted to an extensive annotated bibliography.

914. *Boletín de filología (BFC).* Santiago, 1934–. Title was *Anales* for vols. 1–3. Annual. Published by the Universidad de Chile, Instituto de Filología de la Facultad de Filosofía y Educación, Avenida José Pedro Alessandre 774, Santiago, Chile. Directed by Rodolfo Oroz. Index for vols. 1–9 in vol. 10 (1958) and classified index of articles previously published in vol. 20 (1969).

Text mostly in Spanish, some in German. Articles on Spanish language, especially phonology and grammar. Also includes cultural matters and some Hispanic literature. Book reviews and list of books received.

915. *Boletín de filología española (BFE).* Madrid, 1953–. Quarterly. Published by the CSIC, Instituto Miguel de Cervantes de Filología Hispánica, Duque de Medinaceli 4, Madrid 14, Spain. Directed by Manuel Criado de Val. Indexed in Guerrero.

Text in Spanish. Articles mainly on linguistics and some on literature. Bibliographies of linguistics by subject and country.

916. *Boletín de la Academia Argentina de Letras (BAAL).* Buenos Aires, 1933–51; 1956–. Semiannual. Published by the Academia Argentina de Letras. Distributed by Librart S. R. L., Corrientes 127, Buenos Aires, Argentina. Directed by Roberto F. Giusti. Index of vols. 1–29 (1933–64) in vol. 30 (1965).

Text in Spanish. Articles on Argentine and other Hispanic literatures. Bibliographies on specific literary figures.

917. *Boletín de la Academia Colombiana.* Bogota, 1950–. 5 issues a year. Published by the Academia Colombiana at Carrera 3-A, Número 17–34, Apartado Postal 815, Bogota, Colombia. Directed by Manuel José Forero.

Text in Spanish. Articles, essays, and bibliographic notes on Colombian and other Spanish American (occasionally peninsular Spanish) literatures and languages. Includes some original poetry and news of the academy.

918. *Boletín de la Biblioteca Menéndez y Pelayo (BBMP).* Santander, 1919–38; 1945–. Quarterly. Published by the Biblioteca de Menéndez y Pelayo, Santander, Spain. Directed by Ignacio Aguilera y Santiago. Index for 1919–59 in vol. 26 (1960).

Text in Spanish. Articles and book reviews on language, literature, and ethnology of Spain. Menéndez y Pelayo and classical Spanish writers are frequent subjects.

919. *Boletín de la Real Academia Española (BRAE).* Madrid, 1914–. Publication suspended, 1936–44. 3 issues per year. Published by the Real Academia Española, Felipe IV, Madrid 4, Spain. Index for vols. 1–25 (1914–46) in vol. 25. Publishes *anejos* on linguistics and literature.

Text in Spanish. Scholarly articles on language, lexicology, grammar dialectology, phonology, and literature. Reviews journals and books and lists latest publications.

920. *Books Abroad: A Quarterly Publication Devoted to Articles on Foreign Literatures and Reviews of Foreign Books (BA).* Norman, Okla., 1927–. Quarterly. Published by the University of Oklahoma, Norman, Oklahoma 73069. Edited by Ivar Ivask. Annual index.

Text in English. Contains many short reviews arranged by language and genre, and articles of not more than 4,000 words.

921. *Bulletin hispanique: Annales de la Faculté des Lettres de Bordeaux (BH).* Bordeaux, 1898–. Quarterly. Published by the Universities of Bordeaux, Toulouse, and Poitiers and the Centre National de la Recherche Scientifique, 13, Quai Anatole France, Paris 7, France. Directed by N. Salomon. Indexes for 1899–1928, 1929–48, 1949–58.

Text in French and Spanish. Articles on history, literature, history of ideas, and linguistics. Reviews of books and magazines, list of books received, and bibliography of Hispanic literature.

922. *Bulletin of Hispanic Studies (BHS).* Liverpool, 1923–. Formerly called *Bulletin of Spanish Studies.* Quarterly. Published by the Liverpool University Press. Edited by Geoffrey Ribbans, P.O. Box 147, Liverpool L 69 3 BX, England. Index of vols. 1–30 in vol. 30.

Text mostly in English, some in Spanish. Articles on whole range of Spanish, Portuguese, Catalan, and Latin American languages and literatures. Many book reviews and six-monthly review of journals.

923. *Bulletin of the Comediantes (B Com).* Madison, Wis., 1949–. Semiannual. Edited by James A. Parr, University of Southern California.

Text in English and Spanish. Articles are generally short and deal with the Golden Age *comedia* and earlier drama. Lists current productions of *comedias* and other useful news. Includes current bibliography of foreign publications dealing with the *comedia.*

924. *Casa de las Américas.* Havana, 1960–. Bimonthly. Published by Casa de las Américas, Tercera y G Vedado, Havana, Cuba. Directed by Roberto Fernández Retamar.

Text in Spanish. Articles of broad scope on Latin American social and political matters as well as literature. Also contains excerpts from original works and book reviews.

925. *Clavileño: Revista de la Asociación Internacional de Hispanismo.* Madrid, 1950–57. Bimonthly. Directed by Francisco Javier Conde. Index for 1950–55 (Madrid: Asociación Internacional de Hispanismo, 1955).

Text in Spanish. Articles and book reviews on Hispanic literature and art, reviews of magazines, lists of theses published and in progress, and such special issues as number 42 (1956), devoted to Juan Ramón Jiménez, and number 43 (1957), devoted to Pío Baroja.

926. *Comparative Literature: Official Journal of the American Comparative Literature Association (CL).* Eugene, Ore., 1949–. Quarterly. Published by the University of Oregon, Eugene, Oregon 97403, with the cooperation of the Comparative Literature Section of MLA. Edited by Thomas R. Hart. Cumulative index for 1949–63.

Text mainly in English, occasionally in French, German, Italian, and Spanish. Articles deal with interrelations of literatures, theory of literature, movements, genres, periods, authors, and problems of literary criticism. Book reviews.

927. *Cruz y raya: Revista de afirmación y negación.* Madrid, 1933–36. Directed by José Bergamín. Index of entire set by Rafael Benítez Claros (Madrid: CSIC, 1947).

Text in Spanish. Articles on Spanish literature and philosophy; occasional poetry and short stories.

928. *Cuadernos: La revista mensual de América Latina* (*CCLC*). Paris, 1953–65. Superseded by *Mundo nuevo* (see no. 954). Monthly. Directed by Germán Arciniegas. Text in Spanish. Articles mainly deal with Spanish American literature and events, but some are on Spain. Original poetry and short stories. Various issues devoted to specific countries or literary movements. Many book reviews.

929. *Cuadernos americanos: La revista del Nuevo Mundo* (*CA*). Mexico, 1942–. Bimonthly. Published at Avenida Coyoacán 1035, Mexico 12, D.F., Mexico. Directed by Jesús Silva Herzog. Index for nos. 1–100 (1942–58) published in 1959. Publishes *anejos* on literature.

Text in Spanish. Articles on Spanish American literature, philosophy, and history, with emphasis on contemporary matters. Includes original works and reviews of magazines and books.

930. *Cuadernos de la Cátedra de Miguel de Unamuno* (*CCU*). Salamanca, 1948–. Annual. Published by the Facultad de Filosofía y Letras de la Universidad de Salamanca, Apartado 20, Salamanca, Spain. Directed by Fernando Lázaro Carreter.

Text in Spanish and French. Articles concern the life, works, and philosophy of Unamuno. Bibliography on Unamuno in each issue.

931. *Cuadernos del idioma: Revista de cultura y pensamiento* (*CI*). Buenos Aires, 1965–. Quarterly. Published by Fundación Pedro de Mendoza, Juramento 2291, Buenos Aires, Argentina. Directed by Angel J. Battistessa.

Text in Spanish. Articles, notes, book reviews, and documents on Argentine and other Hispanic literatures and cultures. Also includes bibliography and reviews of journals as well as news about the Fundación Pedro de Mendoza.

932. *Cuadernos de literatura: Revista general de las letras.* Madrid, 1947–50. Superseded *Cuadernos de literatura contemporánea* (see no. 933) and continued by *Revista de literatura* (also see no. 975). Bimonthly. Published by CSIC. Index for entire set in vol. 8 (1950), in Guerrero.

Text in Spanish. Articles on Hispanic literature, book reviews, and bibliographies (often extensive) on all literary genres.

933. *Cuadernos de literatura contemporánea.* Madrid, 1942–46.

Superseded by *Cuadernos de literatura* (see no. 932). Bimonthly. Published by CSIC. Indexed in Guerrero and Tortajada. Text in Spanish. Articles mostly on all genres of contemporary peninsular literature. Reviews of books and magazines.

934. *Cuadernos hispanoamericanos: Revista mensual de cultura hispánica* (CHA). Madrid, 1948–. Monthly. Published by the Instituto de Cultura Hispánica, Ciudad Universitaria, Madrid, Spain. Directed by José Antonio Maravall. Author index for nos. 1–100 in no. 100 (1958).

Text in Spanish. Articles on Hispanic literature, history, and philosophy, especially twentieth-century. Long book reviews, notes on literary events, and special issues devoted to single authors, for example, Azorín (1968) and Galdós (1971).

935. *Cultura neolatina (CN).* Modena, 1941–. 3 issues per year. Published by the Istituto di Filologia Romanza, Città Universitaria, Rome, Italy. Directed by Aurelio Roncaglia.

Text in Italian, Spanish, French, English, and German. Articles on Romance languages and literatures with good representation of peninsular Spanish. Book reviews and list of books received.

936. *Duquesne Hispanic Review: Revista hispánica de la Universidad de Duquesne (DHR).* Pittsburgh, Pa., 1962–. Continues *Estudios* (1951–54). 3 issues per year. Published by Duquesne University Press, Pittsburgh, Pennsylvania 15219. Directed by Reyes Carbonell.

Text in Spanish. Articles on Hispanic literature are contemporary and broad in scope.

937. *La estafeta literaria: Revista quincenal de libros, artes y espectáculos.* Madrid, 1944–. Semimonthly. Published by Editora Nacional, Calle del Prado 21, Madrid 14, Spain. Directed by Ramón Solís.

Text in Spanish. Articles on Spanish literature, art, music, theater, and movies. Also includes such material as book reviews, interviews, and original poetry.

938. *Estudios filológicos.* Valdivia, 1965–. Annual. Published by the Instituto de Filología, Facultad de Filosofía y Letras, Universidad Austral de Chile, Casilla 567, Valdivia, Chile. Directed by Guillermo Araya.

Text in Spanish. Articles on Hispanic literature and philology.

939. *Filología.* Buenos Aires, 1949–. Publication suspended,

1954–58. 3 issues per year. Published by the Ministerio de Educación, Facultad de Filosofía y Letras de la Universidad de Buenos Aires. Directed by Ana María Barrenechea.

Text in Spanish. Articles mainly on linguistics, but some on literature. Book reviews on general Hispanic works.

940. *Filosofía y letras.* Mexico, 1941–58. Published by the Universidad Nacional Autónoma de México. Directed by Salvador Azuela.

Text in Spanish. Articles and book reviews on literature, aesthetics, philosophy, history, and anthropology pertaining to Spanish America, and Mexico in particular.

941. *Germanisch-Romanische Monatsschrift (GRM).* Heidelberg, 1909–. Publication suspended, 1943–October 1950. Quarterly. Published by Carl Winter Universitätsverlag, Lutherstrasse 59, 6900 Heidelberg, West Germany. Edited by F. R. Schroeder.

Text in German. Articles on literature and philology with adequate attention to Spanish. Book reviews, notes, and list of books received.

942. *Hispania: A Journal Devoted to the Interests of the Teaching of Spanish and Portuguese.* Stanford University, Stanford, Calif., 1917–. Quarterly. Published by the American Association of Teachers of Spanish and Portuguese. Edited by Donald W. Bleznick, Department of Romance Languages and Literatures, University of Cincinnati, Cincinnati, Ohio 45221. Cumulative index every 10 years (most recently for 1958–67, published in 1969).

Text in English, Spanish, and Portuguese. Articles devoted to peninsular Spanish, Latin American, and Portuguese literatures and languages. Also contains pedagogical articles and news, general information on literary and cultural events, many book reviews, list of books received, and an annual listing (May issue) of doctoral dissertations completed and in progress.

943. *Hispanic Review: A Quarterly Journal Devoted to Research in the Hispanic Languages and Literatures (HR).* Philadelphia, 1933–. Quarterly. Published by the Department of Romance Languages, University of Pennsylvania, Box 20, Philadelphia, Pennsylvania 19104. Edited by Arnold G. Reichenberger and Russell P. Sebold. Index to vols. 1–25 (1933–57) issued as supplement to vol. 25 (1958).

Text in English and Spanish. Mainly articles on Hispanic and Portuguese literatures, and some on linguistics. Many book reviews on literature and linguistics, and list of books received.

944. *Hispanófila: Literatura, ensayos.* Madrid, 1957–. 3 issues per year. Published at the University of North Carolina, Chapel Hill, North Carolina 27514. Edited by A. V. Ebersole. Cumulative index every 3 years.

Text in Spanish and, occasionally, in English. Articles on Spanish and Spanish American literatures of all genres and periods. Book reviews.

945. *Iberoromania: Revista destinada a las lenguas y literaturas de España, Portugal y Latinoamérica.* Munich, 1969–71; Gottingen, 31 March 1973–. Quarterly and now semiannual. Published at 34 Gottingen, Otfried—Muller Weg 10, West Germany. Printed by Ediciones Alcalá, Madrid. Directed by Dr. Heinrich Bihler (Hans Rheinfelder until 1971).

Text mainly in Spanish, Portuguese, and Catalan but also in German, English, French, and Italian. Articles on Iberian and Latin American linguistics and literatures and information on congresses and new and projected publications.

946. *Imagen: Quincenario de arte, literatura e información cultural.* Caracas, 1967–. Semimonthly. Published by the Instituto Nacional de Cultura y Bellas Artes, Edificio Gran Avenida, Plaza Venezuela, Apartado de Correos 12.497, Caracas, Venezuela.

Publishes articles, interviews, and reviews on all phases of culture, with an emphasis on that of Spanish America. Here, the term "culture" includes literature, ballet, movies, music, art, art exhibits, and the like. It is well illustrated. Often publishes Spanish translations of both critical and creative material. Almost every number contains a supplement devoted to the study of an individual or a topic. Newspaper format.

947. *Indice.* Madrid, 1945–. Monthly to 1968, now semimonthly. Published at Apartado 6076, Montesquinza 24, Madrid 4, Spain. Directed by J. Fernández Figueroa.

Text in Spanish. Articles on literature, art, dance, theater, and the like. Most articles pertain to Spain, some to Spanish America and other countries. Excerpts from literary texts and book reviews. Newspaper format.

948. *Insula: Revista bibliográfica de ciencias y letras.* Madrid, 1946–. Monthly. Published by Insula Librería, Benito Gutiérrez 26, Madrid 8, Spain. Directed by Enrique Canito. Index for 1946–56 published by Insula (1958).

Text in Spanish. Articles on literatures, poetry, theater, and movies of Spain, Spanish America, Europe, and the United States. Many book reviews. Newspaper format.

949. *Kentucky Romance Quarterly (KRQ).* Lexington, Ky., 1967–. Supersedes *Kentucky Foreign Language Quarterly* (1954–67). Quarterly. Published by the University of Kentucky, Lexington, Kentucky 40506. Edited by John E. Keller.

Text mainly in English but also in French, Spanish, and Portuguese. Articles on Hispanic, French, and other Romance literatures.

950. *Latin American Literary Review (LALR).* Pittsburgh, Pa., 1972–. Semiannual. Published by the Department of Modern Languages, Carnegie-Mellon University, Pittsburgh, Pennsylvania 15213. Edited by Espinosa Miller, Carlos Navarro, and Edward Dudley.

Text in English. Articles on the literatures of Latin America and Latin American minorities in the United States. Also includes creative writing and book reviews limited to the analysis of creative works.

951. *Latin American Theatre Review: A Journal Devoted to the Theatre and Drama of Spanish and Portuguese America (LATR).* Lawrence, Kans., 1967–. Semiannual. Published by the Center of Latin American Studies. University of Kansas, Lawrence, Kansas 66044. Edited by George Woodyard and Frederic M. Litto.

Text in English, Spanish, and Portuguese. Articles are historical, critical, or bibliographic in nature. Includes current theater activity, play synopses, works in progress, theater seasons, and festivals. Book reviews.

952. *Modern Language Notes (MLN).* Baltimore, 1886–. Changed title to *MLN* with vol. 77 (1962). 6 issues per year. Published by Johns Hopkins Press, Baltimore, Maryland 21218. Edited by Elias L. Rivers. Indexes for vols. 1–50 (1935) and vols. 51–60 (1946).

Text in English, Spanish, and other modern languages. One issue per year devoted to the Hispanic field, mainly literature. Book reviews dealing with Romance languages and German.

953. *Modern Language Review: A Quarterly Journal Devoted to the Study of Medieval and Modern Literature and Philology (MLR).* Cambridge, 1905–. Quarterly. Published by the Modern Humanities Research Association, King's College, Strand, London WC 2R 2LS, England. Edited by T. J. B. Spencer. Indexes for vols. 1–10 (1905–15), 11–20 (1916–25), and 21–30 (1926–38).

Text in English. Articles and many book reviews on literature and language; several articles per year in the Hispanic field.

954. *Mundo nuevo: Revista mensual de la América Latina (M Nu).* Superseded *Cuadernos* (see no. 928). Paris, 1967–71. Monthly. Text in Spanish. Broad variety of articles mainly on Latin American social problems, contemporary literature and literary events, and art. Book reviews and original works.

955. *Nosotros: Revista mensual de letras, arte, historia, filosofía y ciencias sociales.* Buenos Aires, 1907–34; 1936–43. Monthly. Directed by Roberto F. Giusti. Index for years 1907–43 published as *Compilación especial,* no. 39/42 (1971) of the *Bibliografía argentina de artes y letras.*

Text in Spanish. Articles on Hispanic literature and philology with emphasis on Argentina. Book reviews.

956. *Nueva narrativa hispanoamericana (NNH).* Garden City, N.Y., 1971–. Semiannual. Published at Adelphi University, Garden City, New York 11530. Directed by Helmy F. Giacoman.

Text in Spanish. Articles and book reviews on contemporary Spanish American fiction.

957. *Nueva revista de filología hispánica (NRFH).* Mexico, 1947–. Superseded *Revista de filología hispánica* (see no. 973). Semiannual. Published by El Colegio de México, Guanajuato 125, Mexico 7, D. F., Mexico. Edited by Antonio Alatorre.

Text in Spanish. Articles on Spanish and Spanish American literatures and languages, some Luso-Brazilian. Very extensive bibliography on all literary genres and linguistics. Reviews of books and journals.

958. *Orbis: Bulletin international de documentation linguistique.* Louvain, 1952–. Semiannual. Published by the Centre International de Dialectologie Générale, l'Université Catholique de Louvain, Belgium. Directed by Sever Pop (1952–60) and now A. J. Van Windekens.

Text in French, Italian, Spanish, English, and occasionally other languages. Articles on language and linguistics, dialectology, grammar, and comparative studies in these fields. Bibliographies and reviews of books.

959. *Papeles de Son Armadans (PSA).* Palma de Mallorca, 1956–. Monthly. Directed by Camilo José Cela. Index for nos. 1–57 (1956–60) published in Palma de Mallorca, Spain (1961).

Text in Spanish. Articles and book reviews on Spanish literature; original letters, poems, and short stories.

960. *Plural: Crítica y literatura.* Mexico, 1971–. Monthly. Published by the newspaper *Excelsior, Reforma* 18, Mexico 1, D.F., Mexico. Directed by Octavio Paz.

Text in Spanish. Articles on Hispanic and world literatures, culture, politics, society, art, and so forth. Also includes original poetry and excerpts from books and news of literary events. Newspaper format.

961. *PMLA.* Baltimore, 1884–. 6 issues per year. Published by the Modern Language Association of America, 60 Fifth Avenue, New York, New York 10011. Edited by William D. Schaefer. Cumulative indexes for vols. 1–50 (1935), 51–60 (1945), and 51–79 (1964). MLA publishes annually a 4-volume international bibliography: vol. 2 contains Romance, Germanic, and other modern languages.

Text in English and other modern languages. Scholarly articles on modern literatures and languages.

962. *Primer acto: Revista del teatro (PA).* Madrid, 1959–. Monthly. Published at Velázquez 138, Madrid 6, Spain. Directed by José Monleón.

Text in Spanish. Articles on Spanish and world contemporary theater. Reviews other theater magazines. Articles by playwrights on various aspects of the theater. Publishes original plays.

963. *Prohemio: Revista cuatrimestral de lingüística y crítica literaria.* Madrid, 1970–. 3 issues per year. Sponsored by the CSIC and the Instituto di Letteratura Spagnola e Ispano-Americana. Published by Editorial Planeta, Ponzano 74, Madrid 3, Spain. Directed by Manuel Alvar, Rafael de Balbín, and others.

Text in Spanish. Mostly devoted to contemporary and past Hispanic linguistics and literature in its articles and book reviews, but also covers world linguistics and literatures.

964. *Quaderni ibero-americani: Attualità culturale nella Penisola iberica e America latina (QIA).* Torino, 1946–. Semiannual. Published by the University of Torino, Via Po 19, Torino, Italy. Directed by G. M. Bertini.

Text in Italian and Spanish. Articles on Hispanic literature and comparative Italo-Spanish literature. Includes news of intellectual life of Spain, Portugal, and Latin America. Reviews of books and magazines.

965. *Razón y fe: Revista hispanoamericana de cultura (RyF).* Madrid,

1901–. Monthly. Published by the Padres de la Compañía de Jesús, Pablo Aranda, Madrid 6, Spain. Directed by Tomás Zamarriego Crespo. Indexes for 1901–52 published by Ediciones Fax (1954).

Text in Spanish. Articles on world literatures, but most are on Spain and Latin America. Also includes philosophy, especially Catholic, and its relation to literature, as well as concern with contemporary problems of tradition and progress. Bibliography of world philosophy, religion, and history; and book reviews.

966. *Repertorio americano.* San José de Costa Rica, 1919–59. Directed by Joaquín García Monge.

Text in Spanish. Articles devoted largely to the languages and literatures of Spanish America. More attention to book reviews and notices in the early years. One of the most influential literary reviews of Latin America.

967. *Review.* New York, 1968–. 3 issues per year (since 1972). Published by the Center for Inter-American Relations, Inc., 680 Park Avenue, New York, New York 10021. Edited by Ronald Christ.

Text in English. Articles, reviews, interviews, and news on Latin American literature. Has sections devoted to specific writers, for example, Donoso (Fall 1973), Borges (Spring 1973), and Cortázar (Winter 1972).

968. *Revista de archivos, bibliotecas y museos (RABM).* Madrid, 1871–78, 1883, 1897–1931, 1947–52, 1953–. Semiannual. Published by the Junta Técnica de Archivos, Bibliotecas y Museos, Avenida de Calvo Sotelo 20, Madrid 1, Spain. Directed by Eleuterio González Zapatero. Index for 1871–1957 (1958) published in Madrid in 1959.

Text in Spanish. Articles on Spanish libraries, archaeology, history, music, literature, and language. Book reviews.

969. *Revista de dialectología y tradiciones populares (RDTP).* Madrid, 1945–. Quarterly. Published by CSIC, Instituto Miguel de Cervantes, Departamento de Dialectología y Tradiciones Populares, Duque de Medinaceli 4, Madrid 14, Spain. Directed by Vicente García de Diego. Indexed in Tortajada.

Text in Spanish. Articles on all regions of Spain and their dialects, geography, history, culture, literature, music, religion, folklore, and ethnology. Book reviews.

970. *Revista de estudios hispánicos (REHisp).* Río Piedras, 1928–30; 1971–. Semiannual. Published by the Seminario de Estudios Hispánicos "Federico de Onís," Facultad de Humanidades, Universidad de Puerto Rico, Río Piedras, Puerto Rico 00931. Directed by Eduardo Forastieri.

Text in Spanish. Articles on Hispanic literature, linguistics, culture, folklore, and bibliographies. Book reviews and list of books received.

971. *Revista de estudios hispánicos (REH)*. University, Ala., 1967–. 3 issues per year. Published by the University of Alabama, Department of Romance Languages, University, Alabama 35486. Edited by Enrique Ruiz-Fornells.

Text mainly in Spanish and English. Articles on Hispanic literature. Also reviews journals and books.

972. *Revista de filología española (RFE)*. Madrid, 1914–. Suspended, 1938–40. Quarterly. Published by CSIC, Instituto Miguel de Cervantes, Duque de Medinaceli 4, Madrid 14, Spain. Directed by Dámaso Alonso. Indexes: vols. 1–46 (1963) in vol. 47 (1964); Alice M. Pollin and Raquel Kersten, *Guía para la consulta de la "RFE," 1914–1960* (New York: New York University Press, 1964); in Guerrero. More than 70 *anejos* on Spanish language and literature.

Text in Spanish. Articles on early Spanish literature and language, grammar, and dialects. Reviews of articles in related journals. Annual bibliography of Spanish linguistics, philology, literature, history, poetry, and theater (all early Spanish). Also contains a word index and many book reviews.

973. *Revista de filología hispánica (RFH)*. Buenos Aires and New York, 1939–46. Superseded by *Nueva revista de filología hispánica* (see no. 957). Quarterly. Directed by Amado Alonso.

Articles on Spanish, Latin American, and Portuguese literatures and philology of early times. Extensive bibliographies of peninsular Spanish literature and language. Reviews of books and journals.

974. *Revista de ideas estéticas (RIE)*. Madrid, 1943–. Quarterly. Published by the CSIC, Instituto Diego Velázquez (Sección de Estética), Duque de Medinaceli 4, Madrid 14, Spain. Directed by Diego Angulo Iñiguez. Indexed in Tortajada.

Text in Spanish, occasionally in English and French. Articles and book reviews on aesthetics of art, music, and literature.

975. *Revista de literatura (RL)*. Madrid, 1952–. Superseded *Cuadernos de literatura* (see no. 932). Quarterly. Published by the CSIC, Instituto de Miguel de Cervantes de Filología Hispánica, Duque de Medinaceli 4, Madrid 14, Spain. Directed by Joaquín de Entrambasaguas. Indexed in Guerrero.

Text in Spanish. Articles and book reviews mostly on Spanish literature. Extensive bibliographies that list latest books and articles on Spanish authors and Darío.

976. *Revista de occidente (RO).* Madrid, 1923–36; 1963–. Quarterly. Published at Bárbara de Braganza 12, Madrid 4, Spain. Directed by José Ortega y Gasset in its first period, and by José Ortega Spottorno in the second. Index for 1923–36 published by CSIC in 1952.

Text in Spanish. Articles and book reviews on literature, philosophy, art, history, religion, sociology, and political science. One of the most influential Spanish journals of this century in its first period.

977. *Revista española de lingüística: Organo de la Sociedad Española de Lingüística (REL).* Madrid, 1971–. Semiannual. Published by Editorial Gredos, Sánchez Pacheco 83, Apartado 2076, Madrid 2, Spain. Directed by Francisco R. Andrados.

Text in Spanish, Catalan, and French. Articles mainly on structural linguistics relating to Spanish and other languages. Also includes news of linguistic symposia and the latest research in structural linguistics. Many reviews of books published in England, France, the United States, and other countries. English summaries for the articles.

978. *Revista hispánica moderna (RHM).* New York, 1935–. Quarterly. Published by the Hispanic Studies Program, Columbia University, 612 West 116th Street, New York, New York 10027. Edited by Karl-Ludwig Selig.

Text in Spanish. Articles and book reviews on the modern literature of Spain, Portugal, and Latin America. Extensive quarterly bibliographies on Latin American literature and language ended with volume 34 (1968).

979. *Revista iberoamericana (RI).* Mexico, 1939–. Semiannual. Published by the Instituto Internacional de Literatura Iberoamericana, University of Pittsburgh, 660 AIR Building, Pittsburgh, Pennsylvania 15213. Edited by Alfredo A. Roggiano. Index for vols. 1–15 (1939–50) published in 1954 by the Unión Panamericana.

Text mainly in Spanish. Articles on Latin American literature, notes and documents, bibliographies. Reviews of books and journals.

980. *Revista interamericana de bibliografía; Inter-American Review of Bibliography (RIB).* Washington, D.C., 1951–. Quarterly. Published by the Division of Philosophy and Letters, Department of Cultural Affairs, Pan American Union, 17th Street and Constitution Av-

enue, N.W., Washington, D.C. 20006. Edited by Armando Correia
Pacheco. Cumulative index of vols. 1–15 (1951–65) in vol. 15
(1965).

Text in Spanish, English, French, and Portuguese. Articles
mainly on Latin American literature and literary figures. Also
includes recent information on new publications, authors, and
libraries of Latin America. Bibliographies of books, pamphlets, and
articles recently acquired by the Pan American Library and other
select libraries. Many book reviews and lists of books received.

981. *Revista nacional: Literatura, arte, ciencia (RNM).* Montevideo,
1938–55; 1956–67; 1968. Quarterly. Published by the Academia
Nacional de Letras, Canelones 2869, Montevideo, Uruguay.
Directed by José Pereira Rodríguez. Indexes: vols. 1–24 (1938–43)
in vol. 24 (1943); second period, vols. 1–10 (1956–65) in vol. 11
(1966).

Text in Spanish. Articles mostly on literature of Uruguay and
other Spanish American countries. Book reviews and notes on academic life in Montevideo.

982. *Revista nacional de cultura (RNC).* Caracas, 1938–. Quarterly.
Published by the Instituto Nacional de Cultura y Bellas Artes, Apar-
tado de Correos 20.098, Caracas, Venezuela. Directed by Gloria
Stolk. Index for nos. 1–150 by author, subject, and title.

Text in Spanish. Articles on Venezuelan, other Spanish American, and some Spanish literatures. Also includes comparative studies, culture, short stories, and poetry. Bibliographies of Venezuelan
works and reviews of books in all fields, written in other languages
as well as Spanish.

983. *Revue de linguistique romane (RLiR).* Strasbourg, 1925–. Published by the Société de Linguistique Romane, Palais de l'Université, Strasbourg, France. Edited by Pierre Gardette.

Text mainly in French, some English, German, Italian and
Spanish. Articles and book reviews on Romance linguistics, grammar, lexicology, and phonology. Bibliographies of Romance
linguistics, dictionaries, and glossaries.

984. *Revue de littérature comparée (RLC).* Paris, 1921–. Publication
suspended, July 1940–September 1946. Bimonthly. Published by
Librairie Marcel Didier, 4 Rue de la Sorbonne, Paris 5e, France.
Directed by Marcel Bataillon and edited by B. Munteano. Index
cumulative every 10 years; 1921–50 in 2 vols.

Text mainly in French but some in English, German, Italian, and

Spanish. Articles on comparative literature with Spanish frequent. Bibliographies and book reviews.

985. *Revue hispanique* (*RH*). New York, 1894–1933. Edited by Raymond Foulché-Delbosc (to 1929). Index by tome of vols. 1–80 (1894–1930) in *The Hispanic Society of America's Catalogue of Publications,* by Clara L. Penney (New York, 1943), pp. 31–43.

Text in Spanish, French, English, German, and Italian. Articles and book reviews on Spanish and Portuguese history, literatures, and languages. Also general cultural topics. Bibliographies on language, history, the arts, folklore, and literature.

986. *Romance Notes* (*RomN*). Chapel Hill, N.C., 1959–. Semiannual. Published by the Department of Romance Languages, University of North Carolina, Chapel Hill, North Carolina 27514. Edited by Urban T. Holmes.

Text in English, some French, and Spanish. Short articles, frequently by young scholars, on Romance literatures and languages; many on Spain and Latin America.

987. *Romance Philology* (*RPh*). Berkeley, Calif., 1947–. Quarterly. Published by the University of California Press, Berkeley, California 94720. Edited by Yakov Malkiel.

Text in English, French, Italian, Spanish, Portuguese, and German. Articles and book reviews on Romance linguistics, dialectology, phonology, lexicology, and medieval literary theory. Spanish literature and linguistics appear frequently.

988. *Romania.* Paris, 1872–. Quarterly. Published by Félix Lecoy, 2 Rue de Tournon, Paris 6e, France. Edited by Félix Lecoy. Cumulative indexes for 1872–1901 and 1901–34.

Text mainly in French, but some in English, German, Spanish, and Italian. Articles on Romance linguistics and literatures with good representation for Spanish. Bibliographies of journal articles and book reviews.

989. *Romanic Review* (*RR*). New York, 1910–. Quarterly. Published by the Department of Romance Languages, Columbia University through the Columbia University Press, New York, New York 10025. Edited by Michael Riffaterre.

Text mainly in English; some French, Spanish, and Italian. Articles and book reviews on Romance literatures with occasional articles on Hispanic literature, mostly peninsular.

990. *Romanische Forschungen: Vierteljahrschrift für romanische Sprachen und Literaturen* (*RF*). Frankfurt, 1883–. Publication suspended, 1943–50. Quarterly. Published by Verlag Vittorio Klosterman, Frankfurt am Main, West Germany. Edited by Fritz Schalk. Text in French, Spanish, English, German, and Italian. Articles and book reviews on Romance philology and literatures. Yearly analytical survey of philological studies.

991. *Romanistisches Jahrbuch (RJ).* Hamburg, 1947–. Annual. Published by the Romanisches Seminar and Ibero-Amerikanisches Forschunginstitut of Hamburg University, Hamburg, West Germany. Edited by Hans Flasche, et al.

Text in German, Spanish, French, Italian, and English. Articles and book reviews on Romance philology and literatures with good representation of Hispanic literature and language.

992. *Sefarad: Revista del Instituto Arias Montano de Estudios Hebraicos y Oriente Próximo.* Madrid, 1940–. Published by the CSIC, Duque de Medinaceli 4, Madrid 14, Spain. Edited by J. Llamas. Cumulative index every 15 years.

Text in Spanish, also English, French, German, Italian, and Hebrew. Articles on Judeo-Spanish life, literature, culture, and history. Bibliography on problems of Jewish culture. Reviews of magazines and books.

993. *Sin nombre: Revista trimestral literaria.* San Juan, 1970–. Quarterly. Published by Editorial Sin Nombre, Inc., Apartado 4391, San Juan, Puerto Rico 00905. Directed by Nilita Vientós Gastón.

Text in Spanish. Articles and book reviews on Hispanic literature and news of the literary world.

994. *Sur.* Buenos Aires, 1931–70. Bimonthly. Directed by Victoria Ocampo. Index for nos. 1–302 (1931–66) in nos. 303–5 (November 1966–April 1967).

Text in Spanish. Articles and book reviews on literary studies, mostly Spanish American. Much original work of contemporary Hispanic authors and others (in translation). Bibliographies on contemporary literature.

995. *Symposium: A Quarterly Journal in Modern Literatures.* Syracuse, N.Y., 1946–. Quarterly. Published by the Department of Romance Languages of Syracuse University with the Centro de Estudios Hispánicos, through the Syracuse University Press, Syracuse, New York 13210. Edited by J. H. Matthews.

Text mainly in English, some French, German, and Spanish. Articles and book reviews on many modern literatures with good representation in the Hispanic field. Recent special issues devoted to authors (e.g., Galdós, Summer 1970) and themes (e.g., myth, Summer 1971; and psychoanalytical approaches to literary texts, Winter 1972).

996. *Thesaurus: Boletín del Instituto Caro y Cuervo.* Bogota, 1945–. 3 issues per year. Published by the Instituto Caro y Cuervo, Apartado Aéreo 20002, Bogota, Colombia. Directed by José Manuel Rivas Sacconi.

Text in Spanish. Articles on Spanish American, Spanish, and Colombian literatures, linguistics, grammar, dialectology, phonology, lexicology, and folklore. Reviews of books and leading philological magazines.

997. *La torre: Revista general de la Universidad (Torre).* Río Piedras, 1953–. Quarterly. Published by Editorial Universitaria, Apartado X, Río Piedras, Puerto Rico. Directed by Jaime Benítez. Index for years 1953–60.

Text in Spanish. Articles on Puerto Rican and other Hispanic literatures, philosophy, history, and politics. Bibliography on Puerto Rico, Argentina, Mexico, and Spain. Book reviews on world literatures.

998. *Universidad de la Habana (UH).* Havana, 1934–. Bimonthly. Published by the Departamento de Intercambio Universitario, Havana, Cuba. Directed by Elías Entralgo y Vallina. Index for nos. 1– 124/129 (1934–56) in 1959.

Articles and book reviews on Cuban and other Hispanic literatures, comparative literature, history, philosophy, politics, and culture. More politically oriented since 1958.

999. *Zeitschrift für romanische Philologie (ZRP).* Tübingen, 1877–. Suspended, 1914–23 and 1945–48. 3 double issues per year. Published at 74 Tübingen, Pfrondorfer Strasse 4, West Germany. Edited by Kurt Baldinger. Cumulative indexes for vols. 1–30 and 31–50.

Monographs on linguistics. Text in German, French, Spanish, English, and other Romance languages. Articles and book reviews on Hispanic and other Romance languages and literatures. Bibliographic supplements of literature and linguistics have extremely wide coverage, especially since the publication of the volume for the years 1940–50. With the four-volume bibliography for the years 1961–62, *ZRP* has been publishing its valuable bibliography under the title *Romanische Bibliographie/Bibliographie romane/Romance Bibliography.*

14   Libraries

Guides

1000. Columbus Memorial Library of the Pan American Union. *Guía de bibliotecas de la América latina: Edición provisional.* 2d ed. Washington, D.C.: Pan American Union, 1962 (1942). viii + 166 pp.

Alphabetical arrangement within each country by name of institution. Data given for each: address, name of head librarian, number of volumes in library, date of founding, type of library, and indication whether exchange service provided. Includes general libraries with more than 2,000 volumes and scholarly libraries with more than 1,000.

Downs. *American Library Resources.* See no. 20.

1001. Esdaile, Arundell. *National Libraries of the World.* 2d ed., revised by F. J. Hill. London: Library Association, 1957 (1934). 413 pp.

History, important collections, building description, catalogs, place in national system, staff, and finances are data supplied for each library.

1002. Gropp, Arthur E. *Guide to Libraries and Archives in Central America and the West Indies, Panama, Bermuda, and British Guiana, Supplemented with Information on Private Libraries, Bookbinding, Bookselling, and Printing.* New Orleans, La.: Tulane University Press, 1941. 721 pp.

Libraries, archives, book industry, trade librarians, government appropriations, and historical background are data included.

1003. *Guía de las bibliotecas de Madrid.* Madrid: Servicio de Publicaciones del Ministerio de Educación Nacional, 1953. 556 pp.

Public and private libraries, with addresses, numbers of volumes, and descriptions of manuscripts and special collections.

1004. Hill, Roscoe R. *The National Archives of Latin America.* Cambridge, Mass.: Harvard University Press, 1945. xx + 169 pp.

History, organization, contents, and publications of the 19 existing national archives. Illustrations.

1005. *International Library Directory.* London: A. P. Wales Organization, 1963–.

Thorough listing by country. Description and address of each library.

1006. Martijevic, Nicolás. *Guía de las bibliotecas universitarias argentinas.* Bahía Blanca: Centro de Documentación Bibliotecología; Tucumán: Junta de Bibliotecas Universitarias Nacionales Argentinas, 1970. 171 pp.

Basic information about the holdings of Argentine university libraries.

Catalogs

1007. Aguilar Piñal, Francisco. *Impresos castellanos del siglo XVI en el British Museum.* Madrid: Consejo Superior de Investigaciones Científicas, 1970. 137 pp.

Annotated listing of books which complements Thomas's *Short-Title Catalogue* (see no. 75).

1008. Bancroft Library. *Catalog of Printed Cards.* Berkeley and Los Angeles: University of California Press; Boston: G. K. Hall & Co., 1964. 22 vols.

A photocopy of author and title cards of an important Hispanic collection.

1009. Biblioteca Nacional de Madrid. *Inventario general de manuscritos de la Biblioteca Nacional.* Madrid: Ministerio de Educación Nacional, 1953–62. 8 vols.

Annotated bibliographic descriptions dealing mostly with literature and history.

1010. Bibliotheek der Rejksuniversitiet te Utrecht. *España e Hispanoamérica: Catálogo de libros españoles y publicaciones extranjeras sobre España e Hispanoamérica.* Utrecht: Rejksuniversitiet te Utrecht, 1948–60. 1 vol. + 7 supplements.

Includes linguistics, literature, periodicals, dictionaries, grammars, histories of literature, anthologies, and translations. Foreign entries in languages of sources but annotations in Spanish.

1011. Castañeda, Carlos E., and Jack A. Dabbs. *Guide to the Latin American Manuscripts in the University of Texas Library.* Cambridge, Mass.: Harvard University Press, 1939. x + 217 pp.

Complete listing of manuscripts on the history and culture of

Latin America and of former Spanish colonies now part of the United States.

1012. Florida University Libraries. *Catalog of the Latin American Library.* Boston: G. K. Hall & Co., 1974–. 13 vols.

Lists approximately 120,000 volumes, pamphlets, periodicals, and government documents in their original forms. Greatest strength in Cuban, Haitian, and Dominican Republic materials, but also good in other Latin American materials. Includes, in order of strength, history, social and political sciences, literature, and the other humanities.

1013. Harvard University Library. *Latin American Literature: Classification Schedule; Classified Listing by Call Number; Author and Title Listing; Chronological Listing.* Cambridge, Mass.: Harvard University Press, 1969. 489 pp.

1014. Hispanic and Luso-Brazilian Councils, Canning House Library, London. *Author and Subject Catalogues.* Boston: G. K. Hall & Co., 1967. Hispanic Council, 4 vols.; Luso-Brazilian Council, 1 vol.

This library contains 30,000 Latin American, Portuguese, and Spanish books, mostly of the nineteenth and twentieth centuries. Philosophy, religion, education, history, economics, the arts, and language and literature are among the broad range of cultural areas covered. The library also houses important cultural and economic serials.

1015. Hispanic Society of America. *Catalogue of the Library of the Hispanic Society of America.* Boston: G. K. Hall & Co., 1962. 10 vols. First supplement, 1970, 4 vols.

Photocopies of cards for every book printed since 1700. Manuscripts, most periodicals, and pre-1700 books are not included. Emphasis is on the art, history, and literature of Spain, Portugal, and colonial Hispanic America.

1016. Instituto Nacional del Libro Español. Directed by Lucas Florentino Zamora. *Catálogo general de la librería española, 1932–1950.* Madrid: Instituto Nacional del Libro Español, 1957–65. 4 vols.

Publishers and variant editions, prices, and numbers of pages of 69,575 entries. Books deal with Spanish America, France, Italy, and Spain.

1017. McKnight, William, and Mabel Barrett Jones. *A Catalogue of "comedias sueltas" in the Library of the University of North*

Carolina. Chapel Hill: University of North Carolina Press, 1965. vii + 240 pp.

Author index follows list of plays. Title listing also includes opening and final lines. More than 1,900 items, covering Catalonian and Spanish plays of the Golden Age and the eighteenth century.

1018. Molinaro, J. A., J. H. Parker, and Evelyn Rugg. *A Bibliography of "comedias sueltas" in the University of Toronto Library.* Toronto: University of Toronto Press, 1959. vii + 149 pp.

Seventeenth- and eighteenth-century drama. First entry dated 1703 and last 1825. Lists original title with shortened version of publication's name, first and last printed lines, publisher, date, and number of pages.

Penney. *Printed Books, 1468–1700.* See no. 70.

1019. Regueiro, José M. *Spanish Drama of the Golden Age: A Catalogue of the "comedia" Collection in the University of Pennsylvania Libraries.* New Haven, Conn.: Research Publications, 1971. 106 pp.

1020. Rodríguez-Moñino, Antonio, and María Brey Mariño. *Catálogo de los manuscritos poéticos castellanos existentes en la biblioteca de The Hispanic Society of America (siglos XV, XVI y XVII).* New York: Hispanic Society of America, 1965–66. 3 vols.

Catalog of 248 manuscripts of lyric poetry, divided into three major sections: collections, authors, and anonymous works.

1021. Rogers, Paul P. *The Spanish Drama Collections in the Oberlin College Library: A Descriptive Catalogue.* Oberlin, Ohio: Oberlin College Press, 1940. ix + 468 pp. Supplement, under same title, published in 1946, 157 pp.

Lists 7,400 dramatic works dating from 1678 to 1924. Annotated as to condition of manuscript, notes, cross references, imprint, pagination, size, and series.

Thomas. *Short-Title Catalogue.* See no 75.

1022. Tudela de la Orden, José. *Los manuscritos de América en las bibliotecas de España.* Madrid: Cultura Hispánica, 1954. 586 pp.

Catalog divided into two parts: Madrid, and the provinces. A bibliographic essay is included.

1023. Tulane University. *Catalog of the Latin American Library.* Boston: G. K. Hall & Co., 1970. 9 vols. First Supplement, 1972.

Includes material from all of Latin America, most of which deals with the social sciences and humanities. Specializes in Mexico and Central America.

1024. University of Texas Library. *Catalog of the Latin American*

Collection. Boston: G. K. Hall & Co., 1969. 31 vols. First Supplement, 1971, 5 vols.

The catalog represents 479,000 cards; the supplement, 75,000. In the library's 160,000 volumes dating from the fifteenth century to the present can be found information on virtually any subject relating to Latin America.

1025. Whitney, James Lyman. *Catalogue of the Spanish Library and of the Portuguese Books Bequeathed by George Ticknor to the Boston Public Library.* Boston: Boston Public Library, 1879. Reprint, Boston: G. K. Hall & Co., 1970, 550 pp.

An extensive listing arranged by author. Some 3,200 books and pamphlets in the Luso-Hispanic field are among the nearly 10,000 works.

15   Guides to Dissertations

1026. Chatham, James R., and Enrique Ruiz-Fornells. *Dissertations in Hispanic Languages and Literatures: An Index of Dissertations Completed in the United States and Canada, 1876–1966.* Lexington: University Press of Kentucky, 1970. xiv + 120 pp.

Includes literatures and linguistics of Spain, Spanish America, Brazil, and Portugal. The general index gives a topical analysis of the entries under each of the categories together with names of authors of dissertations and the literary figures to whom dissertations have been devoted.

1027. *Dissertation Abstracts International.* Sec. A, "Humanities." Ann Arbor, Mich.: University Microfilms, 1935–. Vols. 1–11 (1935–51) issued as *Microfilm Abstracts;* vols. 12–29 (1952–June 1969) issued as *Dissertation Abstracts.* The present title began with vol. 30 (July 1969). Monthly compilation.

Contains abstracts of dissertations accepted by most American and Canadian universities and, since 1969, European universities.

1028. *Hispania.* "Dissertations in the Hispanic Languages and Literatures." Vol. 18, 1935–. Published annually in the May issue.

List of completed and in-progress Ph.D. dissertations. Through 1949, M.A. theses were also listed.

1029. Jones, C. A. "Theses in Hispanic Studies Approved for Higher Degrees by British Universities to 1971." *Bulletin of Hispanic Studies* 49 (October 1972):325–54.

Covers the period from 1913 to 1971. The largest number of theses is devoted to literature and history, but such fields as language, Spanish-Arabic studies, education, religion, politics, and economics are also represented. Index of authors.

1030. Kidder, Frederick, and Allen David Bushong, eds. *Theses on Pan American Topics: Prepared by Candidates for Doctoral Degrees in Universities and Colleges in the United States and Canada.* 4th ed. Washington, D.C.: Pan American Union, 1962 (1931). 124 pp. Supplement by Bushong to the *Latin American Research Review* (vol. 2, no. 2 [Spring 1967]), 57 pp.

Earlier editions included master's theses. Lists 2,253 doctoral dissertations.

1031. *Modern Language Journal.* "American Doctoral Degrees Granted in the Field of Modern Languages." Vol. 7, 1922–. Published annually.

Lists currently include dissertations granted in Romance languages and literatures, comparative education, foreign-language education, and linguistics.

1032. Zubatsky, David S. "An International Guide of Completed Theses and Dissertations in the Hispanic Languages and Literatures." *Hispania* 55 (May 1972):293–302.

A very useful annotated list arranged by country or by geographical region, then by type of published list. This list should be the starting point for anyone seeking to find what theses and dissertations have been written in the United States and abroad.

16   Other Useful References in the Hispanic Field

Biographical Dictionaries

1033. Slocum, Robert B., ed. *Biographical Dictionaries and Related Works: A Bibliography.* Detroit: Gale Research Co., 1967. 1,056 pp. Supplement (1972), 852 pp.

Latin American countries and Spain included among the 4,829 references in the basic volume and the approximately 3,500 additional items in the Supplement. Each entry has full bibliographic information and a descriptive annotation. Contains such material as collective biographies, biobibliographies, epitaphs, genealogical works, dictionaries of antonyms and pseudonyms, historical and specialized dictionaries. Indexes of authors, titles, and subjects.

1034. Asenjo, Conrado, ed. *Quién es quién en Puerto Rico: Diccionario biográfico de record personal.* 4th ed. San Juan: Imprenta Venezuela, 1948–49. 216 pp.

1035. Canals, S. Olives, and Stephen S. Taylor, eds. *Who's Who in Spain: A Biographical Dictionary Containing about 6,000 Biographies of Prominent People in and of Spain and 1,400 Organizations.* Montreal: Intercontinental Book and Publishing Co., 1963. 998 pp.

Data include present occupation, date and place of birth, education, career, address, ancestors' awards, memberships, recreation, and family.

1036. Coll y Toste, Cayetano. *Puertorriqueños ilustres.* San Juan, 1967. 372 pp.

Contains 76 biographical sketches selected from the *Boletín histórico de Puerto Rico.* The selection was made by the granddaughter of Coll y Toste.

1037. *Diccionario biográfico de Chile.* 13th ed. Santiago: Empresa Periodística Chile, 1967 (1936). liv + 1,732 pp. 14th ed., 1970.

One of the most complete biographical dictionaries in Latin America.

1038. *Diccionario biográfico de México.* Monterrey: Revesa, 1968. 643 pp.

Provides basic biographical information on prominent Mexican academics and social figures.

1039. *Diccionario biográfico de Venezuela.* Madrid: Blass, 1953. Divided by region or state.

1040. Esperabé Arteaga, Enrique. *Diccionario enciclopédico ilustrado y crítico de los hombres de España.* 2d ed. Madrid: Artes Gráficas Ibarra, 1957. 530 pp.
Around 3,000 entries.

1041. Hilton, Robert, ed. *Who's Who in Latin America: A Biographical Dictionary of Notable Living Men and Women of Latin America.* 3d ed., revised and enlarged. Stanford, Calif.: Stanford University Press, 1946–51 (1935). 7 vols. Reprint, Detroit: Blaine Ethridge Books, 1971, 2 vols.
About 8,000 entries.

1042. Inguíniz, Juan Bautista. *Bibliografía biográfica mexicana.* Mexico: Porrúa and Universidad Nacional Autónoma de México, 1969. 431 pp.
Annotated listing of 1,314 references to books, pamphlets, and periodical and newspaper articles containing biographical data on Mexicans. Includes a name index.

1043. Instituto Nacional del Libro Español. *Quién es quién en las letras españolas.* 2d ed., revised and enlarged. Madrid, 1973 (1969). 548 pp.
Brief biographies of living Spanish authors.

1044. *National Directory of Latin Americanists: Biobibliographies of 1884 Specialists in the Social Sciences and Humanities.* 2d ed. Washington, D.C.: Library of Congress, Hispanic Foundation, 1971 (1966). 684 pp.
Biographies of 2,695 specialists in the social sciences and humanities.

1045. Peraza Sarausa, Fermín, ed. *Diccionario biográfico cubano.* Havana: Anuario Bibliográfico Cubano, 1951–60 (vols. 1–11); and Gainesville, Fla., 1966–68 (vols. 12–14).
Alphabetical biographical dictionary of deceased persons who were born in Cuba or had some connection with Cuba. Volumes 12–14 present new biographies.

1046. ———. *Personalidades cubanas.* Havana: Anuario Bibliográfico Cubano, 1957–65. 8 vols. Vol. 8, *Cuba en el exilio.*
Biographies of living Cubans and those who have had some importance in Cuban life.

1047. *Peruanos notables de hoy.* Lima: Manuel Beltroy, 1958. 202 pp.
Alphabetical biographical dictionary containing complete data on living Peruvians. Index with classification by profession.

1048. *Quién es quién en Colombia.* Bogota: Kelly, 1944–.
1049. *Quién es quién en la Argentina: Biografías contemporáneas.* 9th
ed. Buenos Aires: Kraft, 1968 (1939). 1,083 pp.
    Biographical information for some 8,000 Argentines.
1050. *Quién es quién en Venezuela, Panamá, Ecuador, Colombia.*
Bogota: O. Perry, 1952–.
    Very complete biographical dictionary of living people.
1051. Rosa-Nieves, Cesáreo, and Esther M. Melón. *Biografías
puertorriqueñas: Perfil histórico de un pueblo.* Sharon, Conn.:
Troutman Press, 1970. 487 pp.
    Alphabetical listing of more than 300 biographical sketches of
outstanding Puerto Ricans. Contains bibliography.

Encyclopedias

1052. *Enciclopedia Barsa de consulta fácil.* Buenos Aires, Mexico,
and Chicago: Encyclopaedia Britannica, 1968 (1957). 16 vols.
    Prepared with the advice of the editorial board of *Encyclopaedia
Britannica*. Volume 15 includes atlas, volume 16 guides to further
reading.
1053. *Enciclopedia de México.* Mexico: Instituto de la Enciclopedia
de Mexico, 1966–. 10 vols. Vol. 6 (1972).
    Prepared along the lines of the *Britannica*. Includes all that per-
tains to Mexico in such fields as anthropology, bibliography, biography, science, history, literature, and semantics.
1054. *Enciclopedia dello spettacolo.* Rome: Unione Editoriale,
1954–62. 9 vols. Supplement *Aggiornamento, 1955–65,* published
in 1966 and *Indice repertorio* published in 1968.
    Embraces dramatic and musical theater, movies, and television
from their artistic, social, juridical, and economic points of view.
Covers the "spectacle" from ancient times to present.
1055. *Enciclopedia el Ateneo.* Buenos Aires: Ateneo, 1962–. 6 vols.
    Each volume covers a broad theme: the universe; man, his history
and beliefs; thought and the world of letters; art, music, and spec-
tacles; the world of science; man the builder.
1056. *Enciclopedia universal ilustrada europeo-americana.* Barcelona
and Madrid: Espasa-Calpe, 1907–30; 1930–35; 1934–66. 97 vols.
    One of the most valuable encyclopedias in any language.
1057. *Gran enciclopedia argentina: Todo lo argentino ordenado al-
fabéticamente; geografía e historia, toponomías, biografías, ciencias, artes, letras, derecho, economía, industria y comercio insti-*

tuciones, flora y fauna, folklore, léxico regional. Edited by Diego A. de Santillán. Buenos Aires: Ediar, 1956–64. 9 vols.
A national, not a general, encyclopedia. Biographical entries for Argentinians are numerous.

Handbooks

1058. *Handbook of Latin American Studies (HLAS).* Cambridge, Mass.: Harvard University Press, 1935–47 (vols. 1–13); Gainesville: University of Florida Press, 1951– (vol. 14–). Since 1964, the humanities and social studies have been rotated yearly.

Sections on anthropology, including linguistics, art, education, geography, government, history, international relations since 1830, Latin American language, law, literature, music, philosophy, sociology, travel, and description. Special articles on bibliography collections, archives, and the like. The *Author Index to Handbook of Latin American Studies,* compiled by Francisco José Cardona and María Elena Cardona (Gainesville: University of Florida Press, 1968, 421 pp.) covers volumes 1–28 (1936–66). A subject index is in preparation.

1059. Hilton, Ronald, ed. *Handbook of Hispanic Source Materials in the United States.* 2d ed. Stanford, Calif.: Stanford University Press, 1956 (1942). xiv + 448 pp. Spanish ed., *Los estudios hispánicos en los Estados Unidos* (Madrid: Ediciones Cultura Hispánica, 1957). xiii + 493 pp.

Embraces Spain, Portugal, and Latin America in pre- and post-Columbian times and Florida, Texas, United States Southwest and California until their respective annexations. Describes archives, libraries, museums, scientific societies, works of finished investigations, philanthropic entities or cooperatives interested in progress of Hispanic studies, all up to 1 January 1956.

1060. Sable, Martin H., ed. *Guide to Latin American Studies.* Los Angeles: UCLA Latin American Center, 1967. 2 vols.

Annotated bibliography of text and reference books, government documents, pamphlets, and newspaper articles, mostly in Spanish and English but also in French, German, and Portuguese on all cultural aspects.

1061. ———. *Master Directory of Latin America: Containing Ten Directories Covering Organizations, Associations, and Institutions in the Fields of Agriculture, Business-Industry-Finance, Com-*

munications, Education-Research, Government, International Cooperation, Labor Cooperations, Publishing, Religion, and Social and Social Services Organizations and Associations. Los Angeles: UCLA Latin American Center, 1965. xiv + 438 pp.

Supplies names and addresses of associations, organizations, and institutions with relevance and interest in the 20 countries and Puerto Rico and British, Dutch, and French Caribbean and South Atlantic islands belonging to Spanish American countries.

1062. Véliz, Claudio, ed. *Latin America and the Caribbean: A Handbook.* New York: Frederick A. Praeger; London: A. Blond, 1968. 840 pp.

Collection of brief interpretative essays by some 80 well-known British, United States, and Latin American scholars. Deals with history, politics, economics, and social and cultural backgrounds. Basic bibliographies but no subject index.

Miscellaneous

History

1063. Altamira, Rafael. *Manual de historia de España, desde los orígenes hasta nuestros días.* 2d ed. Buenos Aires: Sudamericana, 1946 (1933). 601 pp. English translation by Muna Lee, *A History of Spain* (Princeton, N.J.: D. Van Nostrand Co., 1949). 748 pp.

A basic general history.

1064. Castro, Américo. *La realidad histórica de España.* 4th ed. Mexico: Porrúa, 1971 (1948). 479 pp. Revised version of his earlier *España en su historia (cristianos, moros y judíos).* English translations, *The Structure of Spanish History* (Princeton, N.J.: Princeton University Press, 1954); and *The Spaniards: An Introduction to Their History* (Berkeley and Los Angeles: University of California Press, 1971).

Important work on the development of the Spanish nation whose character was formed by the symbiotic relationships of Christians, Moors, and Jews in the Middle Ages.

1065. Crow, John A. *The Epic of Latin America.* 2d ed. Garden City, N.Y.: Doubleday & Co., 1971 (1946). xxvi + 879 pp.

From Indian civilizations to the twentieth century, dealing with cultural, economic, literary, and political history of Latin America.

1066. ———. *Spain: The Root and the Flower.* New York: Harper & Row, 1963. 412 pp.

Well-written overview of Spanish history.

1067. *Diccionario de historia de España desde sus orígenes hasta el final del reinado de Alfonso XIII.* Madrid: Revista de Occidente, 1952. 2 vols.

Handy reference work. Useful for world history also. Chronological index, bibliography, and maps.

1068. *Diccionario Porrúa de historia, biografía y geografía de México.* 3d ed., revised and enlarged. Mexico: Porrúa, 1971 (1964). 2 vols. 2,465 pp.

Biographical material on Mexicans or those whose activities have linked them to Mexico.

1069. Griffin, Charles C., and J. Benedict Warren, eds. *Latin America: A Guide to the Historical Literature.* Published for the Conference on Latin American History. Austin: University of Texas Press, 1971. 700 pp.

Selective, scholarly bibliography with 7,087 critical annotations covering Latin American history. Divided into the following sections: reference, general, background, colonial Latin America, Independence, Latin America since Independence, and international relations since 1830.

1070. *Indice histórico español,* 1953–. Quarterly. Published by the Centro de Estudios Históricos de la Universidad de Barcelona through Editorial Teide. Founded by Jaime Vicens Vives.

Contains information on studies relating to the history of Spain from prehistoric times to the twentieth century as well as of Spanish America from the discovery to Independence. Publishes annual author and subject indexes.

1071. Sánchez-Albornoz, Claudio. *España: Un enigma histórico.* 2d ed. Buenos Aires: Sudamericana, 1962 (1956). 2 vols.

A refutation of Américo Castro's *La realidad histórica de España.* Besides criticizing Castro's scholarship, it traces the formation of the Spanish character to the early inhabitants of Spain.

1072. Sánchez Alonso, Benito. *Fuentes de la historia española e hispanoamericana.* 3d rev. ed. Madrid: Consejo Superior de Investigaciones Científicas, 1952 (1919). 3 vols.

A fundamental source for Hispanic historical bibliography.

Philosophy

1073. Ferrater Mora, José. *Diccionario de filosofía.* 5th ed. Buenos Aires: Sudamericana, 1965 (1941). 2 vols.

A remarkable work of more than 2,000 pages by an internationally recognized scholar. Alphabetically arranged, it includes all aspects of world philosophy from classical antiquity to the present. Besides biobibliographic studies and analyses of the works of many philosophers—Hispanic philosophers are extremely well represented—there are entries on philosophical terms, concepts, schools, and movements. Substantial bibliographies accompany most entries.

1074. Martínez Gómez, Luis, S.J. *Bibliografía filosófica española e hispanoamericana (1940–1958).* Barcelona: Juan Flors, 1961. 500 pp.

A comprehensive listing of studies on philosophy. Classified by author and subject. Contains an index of names.

1075. *Repertoire bibliographique de la philosophie.* Supplement to the *Revue philosophique de Louvain.* Louvain, 1949–.

Includes philosophical literature published in German, English, Spanish, Catalan, French, Italian, and Portuguese. Contains general studies as well as studies on individual philosophers organized by historical periods and by countries. Covers books and articles and book reviews in periodicals.

17   Selected Publishers

Information on most presses, in particular United States presses, which publish material of interest for the Hispanist is available in the *PMLA*'s "Directory of Useful Addresses" (September issue) and *Hispania*'s "Publishers' Addresses" (every issue). Other useful tools are: the appendix "Guía de editores," in *Libros en venta* (New York: R. R. Bowker Co., 1964) and four supplements (1964–66, 1967–68, 1969–70, 1971); *Guía de editores y de libreros de España* (Madrid: Instituto Nacional del Libro Español, 1961); *La empresa del libro en América latina: Una guía seleccionada, de las editoriales distribuidoras y librerías en América latina* (Buenos Aires: Bowker Editores Argentina, 1968); and *Publishers' International Directory* (*Internationales Verlagsaddressbuch*), 5th ed. (Munich: Verlag Dokumentation, 1972), pt. 2.

United States and Canada

Barnes & Noble Books (a division of Harper & Row, Publishers). 49 East 33rd Street, New York, New York 10016.

R. R. Bowker Company. 1180 Avenue of the Americas, New York, New York 10036.

Burt Franklin Reprints. 235 East 44th Street, New York, New York 10017.

Cambridge University Press. 32 East 57th Street, New York, New York 10022.

Catholic University of America Press. 620 Michigan Avenue, Northeast, Washington, D.C. 20017.

Columbia University Press. 2960 Broadway, New York, New York 10027.

Cornell University Press. 124 Roberts Place, Ithaca, New York 14850.

Dover Publications. 180 Varick Street, New York, New York 10014.

Duke University Press. Box 6697 College Station, Durham, North Carolina 27708.

Hafner Publishing Company, Inc. 31 East 10th Street, New York, New York 10003.

Harvard University Press. 79 Garden Street, Cambridge, Massachusetts 02138.

The Hispanic Society of America. Broadway between 155th and 156th Streets, New York, New York 10032.

Indiana University Press. 10th and Morton Streets, Bloomington, Indiana 47401.

The Johns Hopkins Press. Homewood, Baltimore, Maryland 21218.

Kraus Reprint Company. Route 100, Millwood, New York 10546.

L. A. Publishing Company, Inc. 40–22 23rd Street, Long Island City, New York, New York 11101.

Louisiana State University Press. Baton Rouge, Louisiana 70803.

New York University Press. Washington Square, New York, New York 10003.

Northwestern University Press. 1735 Benson Avenue, Evanston, Illinois 60201.

Ohio State University Press. 2070 Neil Avenue, Columbus, Ohio 43210.

Penguin Books. 7110 Ambassador Road, Baltimore, Maryland 21207.

Pennsylvania State University Press. University Park, Pennsylvania 16802.

Princeton University Press. Princeton, New Jersey 08540.

Scarecrow Press, Inc. P.O. Box 656, Metuchen, New Jersey 08840.

Southern Illinois University Press. Carbondale, Illinois 62901.

Stanford University Press. Stanford, California 94305.

Syracuse University Press. Box 8, University Station, Syracuse, New York 13210.

Temple University Press. Philadelphia, Pennsylvania 19122.

Twayne Publishers. 31 Union Square, New York, New York 10003.

University Microfilms, Inc. 300 North Zeeb Road, Ann Arbor, Michigan 48106.

University of Alabama Press. Drawer 2877, University, Alabama 35486.

University of California Press. Berkeley, California 94720.

University of Chicago Press. 5801 Ellis Avenue, Chicago, Illinois 60637.

University of Florida Press. 15 Northwest 15th Street, Gainesville, Florida 32601.

University of Georgia Press. Athens, Georgia 30601.

University of Illinois Press. Urbana, Illinois 61801.

University of Miami Press. Coral Gables, Florida 33124.

University of Michigan Press. Ann Arbor, Michigan 48106.
University of Minnesota Press. 2037 University Avenue Southeast, Minneapolis, Minnesota 55455.
University of Missouri Press. Columbia, Missouri 65201.
University of Nebraska Press. Lincoln, Nebraska 68508.
University of New Mexico Press. Albuquerque, New Mexico 87106.
University of North Carolina Press. Box 510, Chapel Hill, North Carolina 27514.
University of Oklahoma Press. Norman, Oklahoma 73069.
University of Pennsylvania Press. 3933 Walnut Street, Philadelphia, Pennsylvania 19104.
University of Tennessee Press. University of Tennessee, Knoxville, Tennessee 37916.
University of Texas Press. Austin, Texas 78712.
University of Toronto Press. Toronto 181, Canada.
University of Washington Press. Seattle, Washington 98105.
University of Wisconsin Press. Box 1379, Madison, Wisconsin 53701.
University Press of Kansas. 366 Watson Library, Lawrence, Kansas 66044.
University Press of Kentucky. Lexington, Kentucky 40506.
Vanderbilt University Press. Nashville, Tennessee 37203.
Yale University Press. 149 York Street, New Haven, Connecticut 06511.

Spain and Spanish America

Aguilar, S.A. de Ediciones. Juan Bravo 38, Madrid 6, Spain.
Alianza Editorial. Milan 38, Madrid 17, Spain.
Casa de la Cultura Ecuatoriana. Avenida Seis de Diciembre, N° 332, Quito, Ecuador.
Casa de las Américas. G. y Tercera, Vedado, Havana, Cuba.
El Colegio de México. Guanajuato 125, Mexico 7, D.F., Mexico.
Consejo Superior de Investigaciones Científicas. Librería Científica Medinaceli, Duque de Medinaceli 4, Madrid 14, Spain.
Ediciones Anaya. Braille 4, Salamanca, Spain.
Ediciones Atlas. Lope de Vega 18, Apartado 840, Madrid 14, Spain.
Ediciones de Andrea. Apartado Postal 32-079, Administración 32, Mexico 1, D.F., Mexico.
Ediciones Destino. Talleres 62, Barcelona 1, Spain.
Ediciones Guadarrama. Lope de Rueda 13, Apartado 14898, Madrid 9, Spain.

Ediciones Rialp. Preciados 44, Madrid 13, Spain.

Editora Nacional. Paseo de la Castellana 40, Madrid 1, Spain.

Editorial Alfa. Ciudadela 1389, Montevideo, Uruguay.

Editorial Castalia. Zurbano 39, Madrid 10, Spain.

Editorial Ebro. Capitán Esponera 18, Zaragoza, Spain.

Editorial Gredos. Sánchez Pacheco 83, Apartado 2076, Madrid 2, Spain.

Editorial Gustavo Gili. Rosellón 87 y 89, Barcelona 15, Spain.

Editorial Joaquín Mortiz. Guaymas 33, Apartado Postal 24-411, Mexico 7, D.F., Mexico.

Editorial Juventud. Provenza 101, Apartado 3, Barcelona 15, Spain.

Editorial Losada. Alsina 1131, Buenos Aires, Argentina.

Editorial Planeta. Calvet 51-53, Barcelona 6, Spain.

Editorial Pleamar. Tucumán 764, Buenos Aires, Argentina.

Editorial Porrúa. Apartado Postal M-7990, Administración 1, Mexico 1, D.F., Mexico.

Editorial Prensa Española. Serrano 61, Madrid 6, Spain.

Editorial Seix Barral. Provenza 219, Apartado de Correos 5023, Barcelona 8, Spain.

Editorial Sudamericana. Humberto 1º 545, Buenos Aires, Argentina.

Editorial Universitaria. San Francisco 454, Casilla 10220, Santiago, Chile.

Editorial Universitaria. Universidad de Puerto Rico, Apartado Postal X, San Juan, Puerto Rico 00931.

Editorial Universitaria de Buenos Aires. Rivadavia 1571/73, Buenos Aires, Argentina.

Emecé Editores. Alsina 2041, Buenos Aires, Argentina.

Espasa-Calpe. Carrera de Irún, Km. 12, Variante de Fuencarral 200, Madrid 20, Spain.

Fondo de Cultura Económica. Avenida de la Universidad 975, Mexico 12, D.F., Mexico.

Instituto Caro y Cuervo. Apartado Aéreo 20002, Bogota, Colombia.

Instituto de Cultura Hispánica. Avenida de los Reyes Catolicos, s/Nº, Madrid 3, Spain.

Insula. Librería de Ciencias y Letras, Carmen 9 y Preciados 8, Madrid, Spain.

Monte Avila Editores. Centro Comercial "Cediaz," Local 5B, Avenida Casanova, Apartado de Correos 20.098, Sábana Grande, Caracas, Venezuela.

Oscar Macchi. Librería Editorial Universitaria, Paraguay 2074, Buenos Aires, Argentina.

Real Academia Española. Calle de Felipe IV, Madrid 4, Spain.

Siglo Veintiuno Editores. Gabriel Mancera 65, Apartado Postal 27-506, Mexico 12, D.F., Mexico.

Taurus Ediciones. Plaza del Marqués de Salamanca 7, Madrid 6, Spain.

Unión de Universidades de América Latina. Apartado Postal 70232, Ciudad Universitaria, Mexico 20, D.F., Mexico.

Universidad Central del Ecuador. Editorial Universitaria, Quito, Ecuador.

Universidad de Costa Rica. Departamento de Publicaciones, Ciudad Universidad de "Rodrigo Facio," San José, Costa Rica.

Universidad de San Carlos de Guatemala. Imprenta y Librería Universitarias 10a, Calle 9-59, Zona 1, Guatemala.

Universidad Nacional Antónoma de Honduras. Centro Universitario de Estudios Generales, Tegucigalpa, D.C., Honduras.

Universidad Nacional Autónoma de México. Departamento de Distribución de Libros Universitarios, Avenida Insurgentes Sur, Nº 299, Mexico 7, D.F., Mexico.

Universidad Nacional de Colombia. Dirección de Divulgación Cultural Publicaciones, Bogota, Colombia.

Universidad Nacional de la Plata. Facultad de Humanidades y Ciencias de la Educación, Departamento de Letras, Calle 6, Nº 775, La Plata, Argentina.

Universidad Nacional de Zulia. Editorial Universitaria, Maracaibo, Venezuela.

Universidad Nacional Mayor de San Marcos. Departamento de Publicaciones, Avenida República de Chile 295, Oficina 508, Lima, Peru.

UTEHA. Avenida Universidad 676, Apartado 1168, Mexico 12, D.F., Mexico.

18   Selected Book Dealers

United States and Canada

Richard Abel and Company, Inc. Box 4245, Portland, Oregon 97208. Has a Foreign Language Approval Plan for Latin America.

Blaine-Ethridge Books. 13977 Penrod Street, Detroit, Michigan 48223. For current and out-of-print Latin Americana published in the United States and Latin America.

Continental Book Company, Inc. 42-78 Main Street, Flushing, New York 11355.

Dosamar of Canada. P.O. Box 1347, Windsor, Ontario.

Johnson Reprint. 111 Fifth Avenue, New York, New York 10003.

Kraus Periodicals and Reprints. Route 100, Millwood, New York 10546.

Larousse and Company. 572 Fifth Avenue, New York, New York 10036.

L. A. Publishing Company. 40-22 23rd Street, Long Island City, New York 11101.

Latin American Book Service. P.O. Box 9505, Rosslyn Station, Arlington, Virginia 22209.

Rizzoli International Bookstore. Spanish Department, 712 Fifth Avenue, New York, New York 10019.

Spanish Book Corporation. 610 Fifth Avenue, New York, New York 10020.

Stechert-Hafner, Inc. 31 East 10th Street, New York, New York 10003.

Eliseo Torres. P.O. Box 2, Eastchester, New York 10709.

Spain and Spanish America

Aguilar, S.A. de Ediciones. Juan Bravo 38, Madrid 6, Spain.

Antigua Librería Robredo. Esquina Guatemala y Argentina, Apartado M-8855, Mexico 1, D.F., Mexico.

Julián Barbazán. Calle de los Libreros 4, Madrid 13, Spain.

Herta Berenguer. Avenida Pocura 2378, Santiago, Chile.

Cámara Latinoamericana del Libro (Latin American Book Chamber). Casilla 15602, Correo 21, Santiago, Chile.

CILA (Centro Interamericano de Libros Académicos). Sullivan 31-bis, Mexico 4, D.F., Mexico. Distributes books of university, academy, and scholarly institutional presses of Latin America.

EDUCA (Editorial Universitaria Centroamericana). Apartado 37, Ciudad Universitaria "Rodrigo Facio," San José, Costa Rica. Publishes its own books and distributes for the Editorial Universitaria of El Salvador, Guatemala, and Nicaragua and for the Universidad Nacional Autónoma de Honduras.

Fernando García Cambeiro. Avenida de Mayo 560, Buenos Aires, Argentina.

Hesperia. Librería Anticuaria, Plaza José Antonio 10, Zaragoza, Spain.

Insula Librería. Benito Gutiérrez 26, Madrid 8, Spain.

E. Iturriaga y Compañía. Jirón Ica 441, Oficina 202, Casilla de Correos 4640, Lima, Peru.

G. M. Kermenic. Apartado Aéreo 90047, Bogota 8, Colombia.

Antonio Lehmann, Librería. Imprenta y Litografía Ltda, Apartado Postal 2014-xi, San José, Costa Rica.

Librería Alfonso Cardenal y Compañía. Apartado 1787, Managua, Nicaragua.

Librería Cultural Salvadoreña. 6ª Calle Oriente 118, San Salvador, El Salvador.

Librería del Plata. San José 358, 1º "A," Buenos Aires, Argentina.

Librería Delta Editorial. Avenida Italia 2817, Montevideo, Uruguay.

Librería Hispanoamericana. Calle González, Nº 1002, Apartado 20830, Río Piedras, Puerto Rico 00928.

Librería Miler. Avenida José Antonio 55, Apartado 1177, Madrid 13, Spain.

Librería Mirto. Ruiz de Alarcón 27, Madrid 14, Spain.

Librería Orfeo. Casilla de Correos 1615, Montevideo, Uruguay.

Librería Porrúa Hermanos y Compañía. Apartado Postal 7990, Mexico 1, D.F., Mexico.

Librería Puvill. Calle Boters, Núm. 10, Barcelona 2, Spain.

Librería Rubiños. Alcalá 98, Madrid 9, Spain.

Librería y Editorial Nascimento. San Antonio 390, Casilla 2298, Santiago, Chile.

Librería y Editorial Universitaria. San Francisco 454, Casilla 10220, Santiago, Chile.

Libros de Colombia (J. Noé Herrera). Carrera 42 C, Nº 22-26, Barrio Quinta Paredes, Bogota, Colombia.

Los Amigos del Libro. Casilla 450 (Calle Perú, Esquina España),
  Cochabamba, Bolivia.
MACH (Mexican Academic Clearing House). Apartado Postal 7-854,
  Mexico 7, D.F., Mexico.
Antonio Mateos Ortega. Gran Librería Anticuaria, Liborio García 11,
  Málaga, Spain.
M. Miranda. León 17, Tienda de Lope de Vega 4, Madrid 14, Spain.
Leonardo J. Muñoz. Loja 396, Apartado 20, Quito, Ecuador.
Passim. Bailén 134, Barcelona 9, Spain.
Porter-Libros. Avenida Puerta del Angel 9, Barcelona 2, Spain.
Fulvio L. Ramírez. O'Leary 1787 y Gelly, Asunción, Paraguay.
León Sánchez Cuesta. Serrano 29, Madrid 1, Spain.
Soberbia. Avenida La Industria, N° 4, Puente Anauco, Caracas 101,
  Venezuela.

Others

E. J. Brill. Oude Rijn 33a-35, Leiden, The Netherlands.
Dolphin Book Company. 1A Southmoor Road, Oxford, England.
European Book Center. P.O.B. 4, Route Henri Dunant 1, 1700
  Fribourg, 2 Bourg, Switzerland.
Otto Harrassowitz. P.O.B. 349, 6200 Wiesbaden, West Germany.
Kraus Reprint Company. 9491 Nendeln, Liechtenstein.
Martinus Nijhoff. P.O. Box 269, The Hague, The Netherlands.
Presses Universitaires de France. 108, Boulevard, Saint-Germain 75,
  Paris VIᵉ, France.
Jean Touzot. 38 Rue St. Sulpice, Paris VIᵉ, France.

Index

Van Tieghem, Paul, 10
Vargas Ugarte, Rubén, 160
Vega, Vicente, 865
Vela, David, 460
Velázquez, Rafael Eladio, 492
Velázquez de la Cadena, Mariano, 854
Véliz, Claudio, 1062
Vergara y Vergara, José María, 441
Videla, Gloria, 330
Vidos, B. E., 765
Villasana, Angel Raúl, 171
Vindel, Francisco, 59
Visca, Arturo, 710
Viscarra Fabre, Guillermo, 635
Vitier, Medardo, 393
Vivanco, Luis Felipe, 305
Vossler, Karl, 223
Vox, 839

Wagner, Max Leopold, 779
Walford, Albert John, 39, 818
Walsh, Donald D., 877
Wardropper, Bruce, 282, 306
Warner, Ralph E., 484
Warren, Austin, 11
Warren, J. Benedict, 1069
Warren, L. A., 229

Watson, Alice G. H., 104
Waxman, Samuel M., 172
Wellek, René, 11
Whitney, James Lyman, 1025
Williams, Edwin B., 855
Williams Alzaga, Enrique, 413
Wilson, E. M., 283
Wilson, Margaret, 284
Winchell, Constance M., 40
Woodbridge, Hensley C., 756

Yahni, Roberto, 179, 629
Yáñez, María Flora, 642
Ycaza Tigerino, Julio César, 485
The Year's Work in Modern Language Studies, 41

Zamarriego, Tomás, 42
Zamora Vicente, Alonso, 258, 780
Zardoya, Concha, 307
Zaunmüller, Wolfram, 819
Zavala, J., 674
Zeitschrift für romanische Philologie, 999
Zimmerman, Irene, 105, 897
Zubatsky, David S., 898–99, 1032
Zum Felde, Alberto, 394–95, 510